Palgrave Macmillan Studies in Banking and Financial Institutions

Series Editor
Philip Molyneux, Bangor University, Bangor, UK

The Palgrave Macmillan Studies in Banking and Financial Institutions series is international in orientation and includes studies of banking systems in particular countries or regions as well as contemporary themes such as Islamic Banking, Financial Exclusion, Mergers and Acquisitions, Risk Management, and IT in Banking. The books focus on research and practice and include up to date and innovative studies that cover issues which impact banking systems globally.

More information about this series at
https://link.springer.com/bookseries/14678

Angela Maria Maddaloni · Giulia Scardozzi

The New Bail-In Legislation

An Analysis of European Banking Resolution

palgrave
macmillan

Angela Maria Maddaloni
European Central Bank
Frankfurt, Germany

Giulia Scardozzi
Roma Tre University
Rome, Italy

ISSN 2523-336X ISSN 2523-3378 (electronic)
Palgrave Macmillan Studies in Banking and Financial Institutions
ISBN 978-3-030-87559-6 ISBN 978-3-030-87560-2 (eBook)
https://doi.org/10.1007/978-3-030-87560-2

Cover illustration: fanjianhua/Getty Images

This Palgrave Macmillan imprint is published by the registered company Springer Nature Switzerland AG
The registered company address is: Gewerbestrasse 11, 6330 Cham, Switzerland

Acknowledgments

The views expressed in this paper are the responsibility of the authors only and should not be interpreted as reflecting the views of the European Central Bank or the Eurosystem.

We are grateful to Franco Fiordelisi, David Marques-Ibanez, Francesco Saverio Stentella Lopes, and Ornella Ricci for helpful comments and suggestions. Francesca Caucci and Pierre Coster provided excellent research assistance support. We would like also to thank all our colleagues and mentors. The authors would like to thank Enago (www.enago.com) for the English language review.

Contents

List of Figures

List of Tables

CHAPTER 1

The New Bank Resolution Framework

Abstract Since the global financial crisis, the European banking industry has experienced great turmoil. European policymakers have implemented a harmonized and enhanced European banking union based on three pillars—supervision (via the creation of the Single Supervisory Mechanism), resolution (via the creation of the Single Resolution Board and the Bank Recovery and Resolution Directive), and deposit insurance. This chapter focuses on the second pillar that introduced the bail-in tool. This tool, introduced with the Bank Recovery Resolution Directive, aims at fostering an orderly and harmonized crisis management in European countries. This chapter highlights the economic mechanisms at work including the possible unintended consequences caused by the change in resolution policy. These include inter alia, political economy hurdles on the implementation, the possibility of runs, and miss-selling.

Keywords Bail-in · BRRD · EBU · Bank resolution

1.1 Introduction

The legacy of the Global Financial Crisis (GFC) of 2007–2009 in Europe was the unraveling of the sovereign debt crises, where investors started

A. M. Maddaloni and G. Scardozzi, *The New Bail-In Legislation*, Palgrave Macmillan Studies in Banking and Financial Institutions, https://doi.org/10.1007/978-3-030-87560-2_1

to differentiate among the credit risk of different European countries, spurred by the very high level of sovereign debt in some countries. One of the main factors increasing sovereign debt was the Government's bailout of several defaulting Too-Big-To-Fail (TBTF) banks using taxpayers' money. Between the beginning of 2008 and October 2014, the European Union (EU) governments approved state aid to their banking systems, amounting to 45.8 percent of their GDP. This state aid comprised €1.49 trillion in capitalization and asset relief programs and €4.3 trillion in guarantees and liquidity measures. Most state aid was in the form of guarantees, some €3.9 trillion in total, and it was granted at the peak of the crisis in 2008. The EU countries decided to form a European Banking Union (EBU), structured in three main pillars, to prevent such a chain of events from happening again in the future and foster orderly crisis management. First, the establishment of the Single Supervisory Mechanism (SSM), according to which, starting from November 2014, the European Central Bank (ECB) is in charge of the direct supervision of the most significant banks in the Euro Area,[1] instead of National Supervisory Authorities (NSAs). The second pillar is the Single Resolution Mechanism (SRM). Based upon the Bank Recovery Resolution Directive (BRRD), the SRM is directly responsible for the resolution process of European banks. In particular, the SRM provides different tools to resolve a bank declared as "failing" or "likely to fail" by the competent authority. Among these tools, the bail-in tool plays a prominent role. The main feature of the bail-in procedure is to impose the costs of a bank resolution primarily on shareholders and creditors of the bank rather than on taxpayers. Among creditors obliged to bear the risk and the cost of a bank failure, bank depositors over €100,000 come last after shareholders and bondholders. This threshold represents the amount that deposit insurance schemes generally guarantee in the European countries. The third pillar of the EBU foresees implementing a common deposit insurance in the euro area, but the process is ongoing.

The regulation framework behind the SRM is outlined in the BRRD, which introduces, among other instruments, the bail-in tool to resolve a distressed bank. We argue that the bail-in is the most radical change to European legislation concerning bank resolution. This tool goes in the opposite direction of resolution strategies implemented after the last

[1] The ECB retains broad responsibility for the supervision of Least Significant Institutions (LSI), while the direct supervision of these institutions is retained by NSAs.

financial crisis (bailout). While the bailout imposes, in fact, bank losses upon taxpayers (due to the state aid provided by the national government to troubled banks); the bail-in requires investors (equity holders, bondholders, and lastly, depositors) to cover bank losses first.

As a consequence of this increase in risk bore by banks' creditors, one might expect investors to ask for higher returns ex-ante to compensate for the higher risk of their investments. This should then translate into an increased cost of funding for banks. Recent literature has analyzed the side effect of the new resolution mechanism on securities issued by banks (see Cutura, 2018; Crespi & Mascia, 2018; Giuliana, 2019). It provides an in-depth analysis of bonds' yields, showing how they increase significantly due to the removal of the implicit guarantee provided by the national government. Similar analysis was conducted by Pancotto et al. (2019) on Credit Default Swap and by Fiordelisi et al. (2020), analyzing stock prices reaction and reaching similar conclusions. At the same time, the broad increase in the cost of funding may have changed the relative priorities between different funding means for the banking sector, seeking to fund itself through cheaper liabilities, the ones better safeguarded by the bail-in hierarchy. This possible change in banks' funding strategy is discussed in Chapter 2. Overall, the increase in funding costs may have caused a change in the liability mix of EU banks with a possible increase in liquidity risk. Implementing the bail-in instrument might have incentivized moving from more expensive (after the introduction of the bail-in resolution) sources of funding for banks (e.g., bonds) toward less expensive sources of funding for banks (e.g., deposits), which are generally short-term. The increase in the volume of short-term liabilities, like deposits, increases the liquidity risk.

As a consequence of the new resolution policy, the higher risk perceived by investors might have had another important implication for the financial market: The allocation of bonds could have changed across the different investors' categories. Over the last decade, there have been several scandals in Europe linked to security mis-selling. In most cases, mis-selling scandals involved risky securities (subordinated debt and junior liabilities) issued by banks and sold to "unsophisticated" investors (households and retail investors), rather than to "institutional" investors. The new resolution regime aims also at improving market discipline and financial stability. The bail-in improves market discipline by limiting the occurrence of moral hazard and imposing the losses on investors; however, there is a substantial risk that retail investors might lose their wealth if bail-in resolution mechanisms are applied on securities that they hold. From a consumer protection point of view, bail-inable securities should not be directed to retail investors, but rather to the banking sector itself, which is rather more sophisticated (de Dreu & Bikker, 2012). At the same time, a bank's investments in other banks' bail-inable bonds may hinder financial stability through a contagion effect that might culminate into a systemic crisis. Pigrum et al. (2016) study the holders of these bail-inable securities through a post qualitative analysis. The analysis finds that the home bias (e.g., holding of bonds by the holders located in the same country of the issuer) plays a role, but, at the same time, they show that non-Euro Area residents held around 40% of bail-inable securities outstanding. Such foreign holding highlights financial stability concerns due to contagion risk. One-third of the holdings are by the Euro Area banking sector, which provides intra-sector validity for the contagion effect. The other major holder of bail-inable bonds is the household sector, which calls for greater enforcement of consumer protection by the regulators. Bekaert and Breckenfelder (2019) confirm the results. They evaluate bank risk allocation with sample data from 2013 to 2018 and use the inclusion of a bank into the list of systemically important banks as an exogenous shock. They find a decrease in bond prices issued by banks included in the list of systemically important banks (therefore subjected to more stringent supervision) relative to the others.

Chapters 3 and 4 examine the allocation of bonds across sectors before and after the launch of the new resolution tool (Chapter 3) and before and after four resolution cases that happened in 2017 in Spain and Italy (4). The analysis is based on a confidential database of the ECB, which stores each security's nominal amount held by each category of investors over time. The analysis shows that the new European banking resolution regime reduced the scope for mis-selling of securities, which had been more prevalent, especially after the GFC. At the same time, the analysis presented in Chapter 4 shows a potential concern for financial stability arising from the increase of bank bonds holdings by the banking sector.

The credibility of the bail-in application has a great deal of relevance. Only if the bail-in is perceived as credible can the new resolution regime improve the market discipline (Philippon & Salord, 2017). The various episodes of bailout resolutions and the potential downsides of the bail-in implementation may undermine the credibility of the new resolution tool. Shafer et al. (2016) analyze the credibility of bail-in by looking at

CDS premia. They find stronger reactions when the bail-in mechanism is actually implemented compared to the announcement or approval of the bail-in regulation. Moreover, many scholars criticized the bail-in tool, arguing that this resolution is still difficult to apply for those banks labeled TBTF. TBTF banks are those banks too big to be left to fail due to the consequent potential systemic crises caused by their failure. TBTF banks had an implicit government guarantee until the BRRD publication. Chapter 4 discusses more recent cases of bank distress in the Euro Area (e.g., Banco Popular and the Italian "Venetian Banks") and how they have affected the credibility of the bail-in resolution tool.

Finally, Chapter 5 analyzes the financial market reactions to cases of bank resolution, providing a comprehensive analysis of the different effects of the implementation of the two main types of resolution mechanism (bailout and bail-in). The recorded effects depend on whether the BRRD had been already approved and the specificity linked to the country in which the resolution occurred.

To resume, the book is structured as follows. The remainder of this chapter illustrates the EBU process with a focus on the new resolution framework. Chapter 2 compares the banks' liability mix before and after the launch of the new resolution mechanism. Chapters 3 and 4 analyze the bond allocation among categories of investors. Finally, Chapter 5 presents the market reactions to bank failures, comparing reactions following actual resolution cases (bailout and bail-in types) over different periods of time and in different countries.

1.2 The European Banking Union

The 2007–2009 financial crisis highlighted the need for a framework of orderly crisis management: From the Lehman Brothers' collapse, many financial institutions were resolved by national governments in different countries. In Europe, the sovereign debt crisis brought policymakers to realize the need to harmonize resolution procedures across the European financial banking system. The bailouts of failing banks by national governments increased public debt levels and spurred market tensions, especially for the government bonds issued by a sovereign with a high level of debt. In 2012, the European Council paved the way for the realization of a banking union in the EU to restore financial stability. Mario Draghi (at the time President of the ECB) referred to the European Commission that "*The economic policies of Euro Area countries are, ultimately, domestic policies for the Euro Area. Precisely because of spill-over effects, they must be subject to mutual surveillance and corrected if required in the collective interest of the Euro Area as a whole. This should apply both to fiscal and macroeconomic policies. [...] National supervisors and Treasuries are also confronted with the well-known problem that during good times, large banks work as European institutions but in bad times fall on national shoulders. Ensuring a well-functioning EMU implies strengthening banking supervision and resolution at European level*" (Draghi, 2012). A few months later, in September 2012, the European Commission (EC, thereinafter) published a draft road map for creating a banking union and assigning powers of supervision to the ECB via the SSM. The European Council adopted the SSM Regulation in October 2013, implemented on November 4, 2014. As of that date, the ECB is in charge of the supervision of European banks as the SSM became operational. Specifically, the SSM directly supervises those banks listed as significant by the ECB, while NSAs supervise the remaining banks in coordination with the ECB. The criteria to be classified as a Significant Institution (SI) are the following:

- Total assets greater than €30 billion;
- Economic importance for the specific country or the EU economy as a whole;
- Total assets greater than €5 billion; the ratio of cross-border assets over cross-border liabilities to Total assets over total liabilities is above 20% in more than one other participating Member State; and
- The bank has requested or received funding from the European Stability Mechanism or the European Financial Stability Facility.

Figure 1.1 summarizes the criteria above mentioned. The ECB publishes the list of SIs annually. This is the first pillar of the Banking Union.

The second pillar of the EBU concerns the resolution procedures for European banks through the SRM. In 2014, the BRRD was endorsed by the EC. The directive prescribed the tools available for the Single Resolution Board (SRB) to resolve financial institutions declared by the ECB failing or likely to fail. The directive became effective in 2015 (except for the bail-in provision which entered into force in 2016). Hence, from 2015, the resolution of European banks is managed by the SRB.

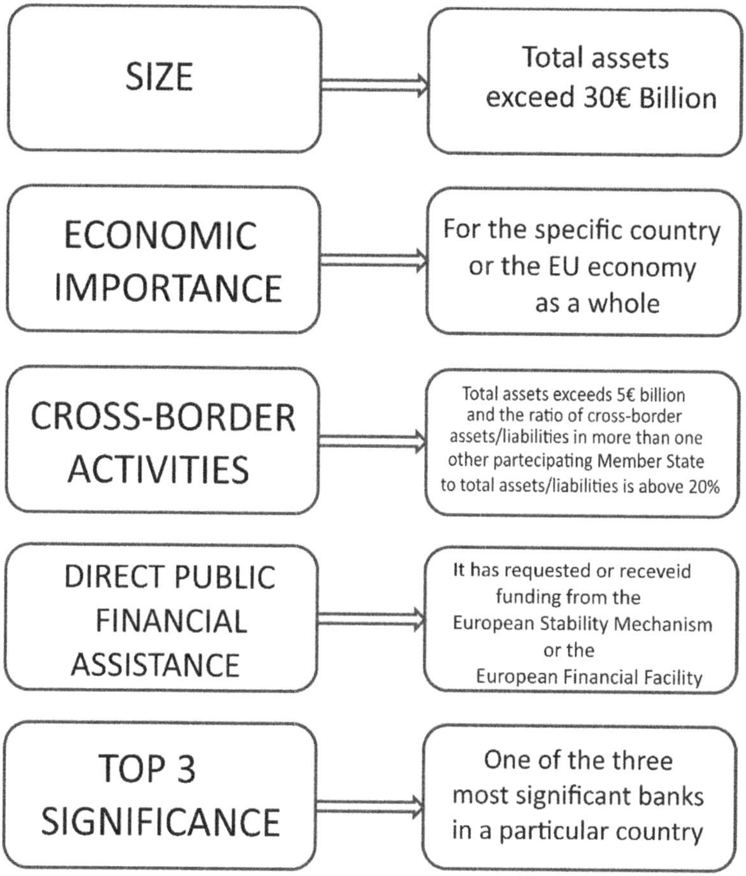

Fig. 1.1 Criteria for Significant Bank classification (*Note* The figure reports the criteria according to which the ECB classifies a bank as a Significant Institution, hence supervised by the Single Supervision Mechanism. The criteria are mutually exclusive: only one of the following criteria is enough to be classified as a Significant Institution. *Source* Authors' own using information from ECB, Banking Supervision)

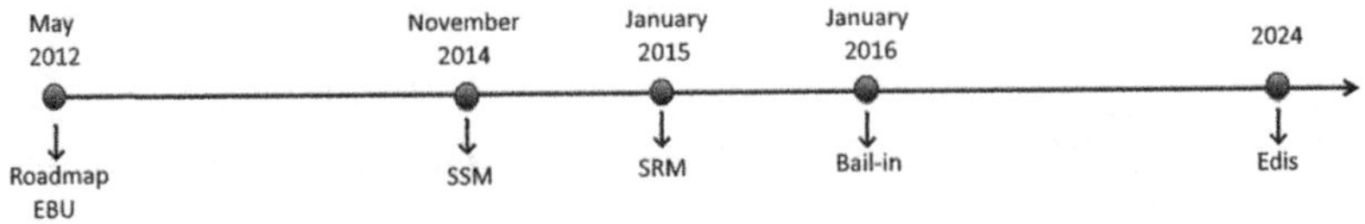

Fig. 1.2 Timeline of European Banking Union project (*Note* The figure reports the European Banking Union (EBU) project timeline, starting in May 2012. Then the figure shows the years in which the three pillars of EBU entered into force: the Single Supervision Mechanism (SSM) in November 2014, the Single Resolution Board (SRB) in January 2015 (except the bail-in tool that became effective in January 2016), and the European Deposit Insurance Scheme (EDIS) still in development. *Source* Authors' own)

Finally, the third pillar of the EBU concerns the European Deposit Insurance Scheme regulation (EDIS, thereinafter). This regulation, proposed in November 2015, will work in combination with the national Deposit Guarantee Schemes. These schemes already ensure bank deposits up to €100,000, which are generally protected in all EU countries. The EDIS would harmonize the deposit insurance over the Euro Area, further enhancing depositors' protection and avoiding bank panic and bank runs. Thanks to the EDIS framework, the level of deposit insurance would not be dependent on the countries in which banks operate. The EDIS is structured in three stages: the first stage of "re-insurance," set to last until 2020; the second stage of "co-insurance," from 2020 until 2024; the third stage of "full insurance," to be operational as of 2024, in which the EDIS would completely replace the national schemes and would be the sole insurance scheme for deposits across Euro Area banks.

The operationalization of the EBU is taking some time to complete (Fig. 1.2), due to the radical changes it requires. However, the harmonization of financial regulation will further consolidate the role of the European Banking System in the global financial system.

1.3 The Bank Recovery and Resolution Directive

The Bank Recovery and Resolution Directive, BRRD (2014/59/EU), has been approved on May 15, 2014, by the European Parliament and the European Council. The directive establishes a framework for the recovery and resolution of credit institutions. It aims to provide authorities with efficient tools to deal with failing banks and pre-defined cooperation arrangements to face cross-border failures. The rationale behind the BRRD is to ensure continuity of the banks' critical functions, transfer losses to investors, and enhance financial stability. The changes in the resolution mechanisms imply an orderly crisis management procedure, common for all Euro Area banks. The directive prescribes four different tools to resolve financial institutions, limiting consequences on financial stability and minimizing the impact of banks failures on public finances and, consequently, on taxpayers. The BRRD states that the SRB is in charge of the resolution procedure of a Euro Area bank. At the same time, the directive establishes a fund, the Single Resolution Fund (SRF), financed by the Euro Area banks to support failing financial institutions. In a broader sense, the directive enhances the authority to tackle banking crises, firstly via an early intervention (when the bank fails to meet its capital requirements), and via a resolution procedure common to all Euro Area banks when the first option is no longer viable. In the case of early interventions, the BRRD grants to the resolution authority the powers to intervene before the bank's condition deteriorates up to the point that it can no longer operates. According to the going concern principle, the resolution authority can require the bank to draw up a recovery plan, change the bank's management, and appoint temporary administrators. In the second stage, the BRRD establishes the resolution of those banks that cannot recover through early intervention. According to the directive, the SRB has four different resolution tools:

- The sale of business;
- The bridge institution;
- Asset separation;
- The bail-in.

The sale of a business tool enables the resolution authority to sell the whole financial institution (or parts of its business) to another institution without the consent of shareholders. The bridge institution tool gives the power to the resolution authority to transfer shares, assets, and liabilities of the failing bank to a bridge institution, which is temporary and partially or totally publicly owned. The asset separation tool enables the resolution authority to separate good assets from bad assets to be transferred to a publicly owned asset management vehicle. The asset separation tool must be used in combination with at least another resolution tool to maximize proceeds. Finally, the bail-in tool prescribes a hierarchy (also known as bail-in hierarchy) of the types of instruments converted into shares or written down, moving the burden of losses from taxpayers (bailout) to shareholders and creditors of the distressed financial institution. All these tools entered into force in January 2015, except for the bail-in tool, implemented one year later (January 2016). This fourth tool represents the greatest change in European legislation concerning the resolution procedures.

It is sensible to argue that these new resolution tools require a framework in which their actual implementation is feasible. Considering, for instance, the bail-in tool, its operationalization requires that the distressed banks have enough equity and debt to be used to cover bank losses. To address this need the BRRD establishes the Minimum Requirement for Eligible Liabilities (MREL). The MREL allows the distressed bank to continue operating as long as it has enough assets to be used in case of resolution. The MREL provision entered into force on January 1, 2017.

Essentially, the BRRD transfers the burden of bank losses, establishing that the costs will be borne first by bank equity holders, then by bank investors, according to the bail-in tool hierarchy, and, only at that point, financed from a resolution fund. Specifically, the resolution fund can be used only after the bail-in of shareholders and creditors for a minimum amount of 8% of a bank's total liabilities has been carried out. It can finance up to 5% of the bank's total liabilities. Only in extraordinary cases when an extensive bail-in might hinder financial stability, the resolution authority might seek funding from alternative financing sources, such as recourse to public support. This eventuality needs to be approved by the EC and only after the bail-in of shareholders and creditors in the measure of 8% of the bank's total liabilities has taken place.

Concerning the SRF, each member state must set up an ex-ante resolution fund financed by the banking sector. Banks' annual contributions are based on their liabilities and the risks they take. The aim is to reach, by 2025, at least 1% coverage for deposits of all credit institutions operating in each country. The fund can be used only if the losses under the bail-in procedure exceed those that shareholders and creditors can bear under insolvency procedures. It will be fully operative only from 2025 (10 years after the new European resolution legislation entered into force).

1.4 The Bail-in Tool

Among the resolution tools provided by the BRRD, the most relevant one, according to both scholars and policymakers, is the bail-in tool. Before the BRRD, national governments provided liquidity injections to restore failing banks; from 2008 to 2014, half of the European GDP was directed into state aid programs for banks. Sovereign debt levels sore as the result, among other factors, of the several bailouts implemented after the 2007–2009 financial crisis. The bail-in tool aims, among other things, to limit the sovereign bank nexus, moving the burden of losses from taxpayers to shareholders and creditors. Specifically, the BRRD establishes a creditors' hierarchy (Fig. 1.3) for the liabilities that fall within the scope of the bail-in. The first level of instruments to be called to cover the losses,

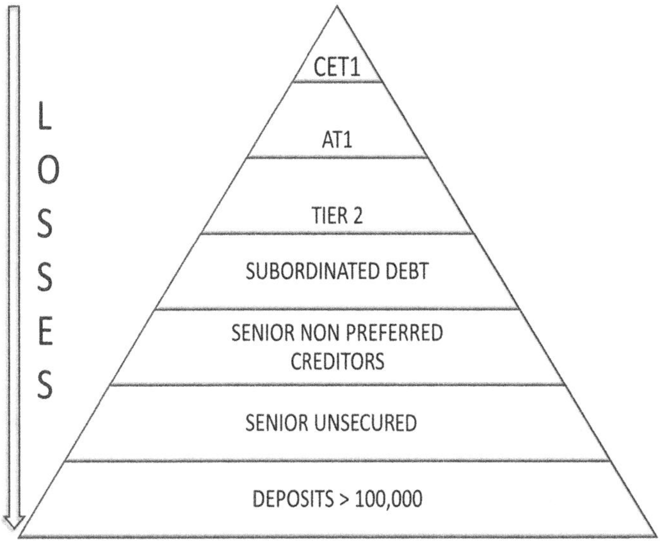

Fig. 1.3 Bail-in hierarchy (*Note* The figure reports the order of security callout by the bail-in tool in case of bankruptcy. At the top of the hierarchy for participation to bank losses, there are the equity instruments. The second macro-category includes the bonds. Finally, at the bottom of the hierarchy, there are the deposits, the last to be called to cover bank losses. The national deposit insurance scheme insures deposits under 100,000 Euros. *Source* Authors' own)

in case of resolution, is the Common Equity Tier 1, followed by Additional Tier 1 and Tier 2. If these instruments are insufficient to cover the losses, subordinated debt and senior unsecured debt[2] will be called upon.

At the bottom of the creditors' hierarchy, there are eligible customer deposits greater than €100,000. Customer deposits smaller than €100,000 are fully protected by deposit insurance, whose harmonization becomes effective within the third pillar of the EBU. Following this hierarchy, the cost of failure is covered by banks' investors, representing the greatest innovation to the European banking legislation. There are, however, at least two different dimensions to consider when assessing this regulatory change. On the one hand, bail-in establishes that public finances will no longer be used to resolve banks causing increases in sovereign debt. On the other hand, the bail-in restricts the number of people who bear the cost of failure, generating large losses for the bank's investors. This, in turn, can hinder financial stability by increasing the likelihood of bank panic and bank runs.

From a macro point of view, the objective of the bail-in is to ultimately improve the market discipline by imposing the losses of a bank on its investors. This should foster an adequate level of market discipline among these investors. Restoring market discipline is necessary because of the benefits of implicit guarantees previously granted to European banks, especially those considered TBTF. The removal of the implicit guarantee seeks, precisely, to restore the market discipline in the banking system and mitigate the risk of moral hazard.

The implementation and application of the bail-in regulation may have several consequences for the banking sector and for the economy. A potential increase in the cost of funding might be one of the most serious side effects of the change in resolution policy. Since banks' liabilities become riskier after the introduction of the bail-in, banks' creditors might require higher returns for their investments, and, consequently, this may translate into an overall increase in the cost of funding. The increase in the

[2] Some countries found that there was ambiguity on the instruments classified as senior unsecured debt, as different types of debt were classified as equally risky by the BRRD. Some countries—such as Germany, France, Italy, and Spain—to better comply with the principle of "no creditors worse-off" set by the directive, decided to integrate the BRRD into their national legislation with a further sub-classification of the category "senior unsecured debt" (Pigrum et al., 2016). The principle mentioned above claims, in fact, that no creditors should suffer greater losses than the ones suffered according to the national legislation of the country in which the securities were issued.

riskiness of bank liabilities depends on the bail-in hierarchy. Hence subordinated bondholders, for instance, might require much greater returns than senior bondholders. Overall, the bail-in hierarchy could generate a change in the funding strategies of the European banking sector, an issue discussed in Chapter 2.

The very clear definition and ranking of all the instruments eligible for bail-in provided by the resolution regulation, fosters financial stability through a better awareness by the bank creditors about the instruments' level of risk. Policymakers aimed to increase such awareness to remedy mis-selling, a phenomenon that will be extensively discussed in Chapters 3 and 4. Retail investors would not retain risky instruments when become conscious of the instruments' actual level of risk clearly stated by the BRRD. At the same time, acknowledging the increase in risk in some bank instruments may increase the likelihood that financial instability is transmitted across financial intermediaries through contagion. Indeed, the increase in holdings of bail-inable bonds by other banks, which are professional investors and therefore able to retain the risk, might hinder financial stability via a cascade effect due to the potential failure of those banks holding the bonds issued by the distressed banks. A proper assessment of the trade-offs involved by this risk-shifting across different sectors is not obvious ex-ante.

Chapter 5 provides some empirical evidence on the market reactions to the policy interventions by differentiating among resolution tools, time of resolution (e.g., before/after the change in regulation), and the banks' location.

Finally, for the bail-in to generate the benefits previously highlighted—enhancing market discipline, reducing moral hazard, mitigating the mis-selling, and enhance financial stability, the implementation of the procedure should be credible. Market participants should believe in its applicability in case of a bank failure. Concerns about the credibility of the tool have been raised, especially in case the failure would involve a TBTF institution (Volz & Wedow, 2011).

1.5 Conclusion

The GFC of 2007–2009 induced distress of many European banks. The consequent governments' bailouts of several defaulting TBTF banks using taxpayers' money in turn strengthened the sovereign bank nexus which was one of the main factors bringing to the sovereign debt crisis. In

Europe, the sovereign debt crisis brought policymakers to realize the need to harmonize bank resolution procedures. The EU fostered the establishment of a EBU, structured in three main pillars, to foster financial stability via orderly crisis management.

The three pillars include the establishment of the SSM, which centralizes the supervision of the most significant banks in the Euro Area. The second pillar is constituted by the SRM, that is directly responsible for the resolution process of European banks. The third pillar of the EBU foresees implementing a common deposit insurance, but the process is still ongoing.

The regulation framework behind the SRM is outlined in the BRRD. The directive provides four tools to resolve a bank declared as "failing" or "likely to fail" by the ECB. Among these tools, the bail-in tool plays a prominent role. The bail-in imposes the costs of a bank resolution primarily on shareholders and creditors rather than on taxpayers. The directive establishes a fund (the SRF), financed by the Euro Area banks to support failing financial institutions. The fund can be used only after the bail-in of shareholders and creditors for a minimum amount of 8% of a bank's total liabilities has been implemented, and it can finance up to 5% of the bank's total liabilities.

The bail-in tool can be considered the most radical change realized to European legislation concerning bank resolution. Under the new regime, only in extraordinary cases, when an extensive bail-in might hinder financial stability, the resolution authority might seek funding from alternative financing sources, such as recourse to public support (bailout).

The rationale behind the implementation of the bail-in resolution tool is to weaken the sovereign bank nexus and foster market discipline. There is some limited evidence that indeed the implementation of the bail-in tool has supported these objectives, partly due to the short time frame and the limited cases in which the tool was actually applied. At the same time, there are other side effects of the bail-in tool that can be identified, relating in particular to banks' choices of the liability mix and the allocation of banks' securities across different investors. Also, the impact on the stability of the financial sector has to be carefully assessed, since the bail-in restricts the number of people who bear the cost of failure, generating large losses for the bank's investors and possibly also increasing the likelihood of investors' runs on banks' securities. In the next chapters, we will analyze some of the collateral effects generated by the launch of the bail-in mechanism and evaluate possible consequences.

References

Bekaert G., & Breckenfelder, J. (2019). The (re)allocation of bank risk. https://dx.doi.org/10.2139/ssrn.3440929

Crespi, F., & Mascia, D. (2018). Bank funding strategies. *Palgrave Macmillan Studies in Banking and Financial Institutions.*

Cutura, J. (2018). Debt holder monitoring and implicit guarantees: Did the BRRD improve market discipline? *SAFE Working Paper Series n.232.*

de Dreu, J. A., & Bikker, J. (2012). Investor sophistication and risk taking. *Journal of Banking and Finance, 36*, 2145–2156.

Draghi, M. (2012). Hearing at the committee on economic and monetary affairs of the European Parliament: Introductory statement. Speech, Frankfurt, European Central Bank.

Fiordelisi, F., Minnucci, F., Previati, D., & Ricci, O. (2020). Bail-in regulation and stock market reaction. *Economic Letters, 186.*

Giuliana, R. (2019). Impact of bail-in on banks bond yields and market discipline. https://dx.doi.org/10.2139/ssrn.2935259

Pancotto, L., Gwilyim, O., & Williams, J. (2019). The European bank recovery and resolution directive: A market assessment. *Journal of Financial Stability, 44.*

Philippon, T., & Salord, A. (2017). Bail-ins and bank resolution in Europe: A progress report. *Geneva Reports on the World Economy Special Report, 4.*

Pigrum, C., Reininger, T., & Stern, C. (2016). Bail-in: Who invests in noncovered debt securities issued by Euro Area banks? *Financial Stability Report, 32*, 101–119.

Shafer, A., Schnabel, I., & di Mauro, B. W. (2016). Bail-in expectations for European banks: Actions speak louder than words. *ESRB Working Paper Series.*

Volz, M., & Wedow, M. (2011). Market discipline and too-big-to-fail in the CDS market: Does banks' size reduce market discipline? *Journal of Empirical Finance, 18*, 195–210.

CHAPTER 2

Bank Funding Strategies After Bail-in Announcement

Abstract The introduction of the bail-in might have induced a radical change in the funding strategy of banks. Changes in the legal protection of funding instruments can have implications for the cost and composition of banks' liabilities. In particular, the introduction of the bail-in mechanism implies an increase in the credit risk of banks' bondholders. Empirical evidence shows that, after the launch of the bail-in mechanism, banks privileged funding via customer deposits—the cheapest source of funding. This may enhance the liquidity risk due to asset-liability mismatch as customer deposits are the source of funding with the shortest maturity.

Keywords Bank deposits · Bail-in · Bank funding · Liability mix

2.1 Introduction

The new resolution regime and, more specifically, the bail-in provision, removed the implicit public guarantee. Bailouts are no longer allowed under the second pillar of the European Banking Union as banks' investors have to internalize and cover the losses of stressed banks. This change in resolution policy implies greater risk-taking for the holders

A. M. Maddaloni and G. Scardozzi, *The New Bail-In Legislation*, Palgrave Macmillan Studies in Banking and Financial Institutions, https://doi.org/10.1007/978-3-030-87560-2_2

of banks' liabilities. Specifically, the effect of the new bail-in regime on bank liabilities is twofold: the yield of outstanding securities issued by banks tend to increase (Cutura, 2018), resulting in a higher cost of funding for banks. This, in turn, might lead to changes in the composition of banks' liabilities. Most analyses focused on market reactions. Some papers have used event studies focusing on stock returns and CDS spreads around the announcements of the various steps of the bail-in regime implementation. They find that the events referring to the implementation of the bail-in caused a greater drop in CDS value compared to the events concerning the announcement or approval of the directive (Shafer et al., 2016). In particular, some studies implemented a difference-in-difference analysis. They compared prices and yields of those bonds that were affected and those that were not affected by the new regulation, highlighting an overall increase in the cost of funding for Euro Area banks (Crespi & Mascia, 2018; Giuliana, 2019). The increase in the cost of funding also resulted in changes in the banks' liability mix. After the bail-in regulation came into force, banks needed to offer investors higher yields, higher coupons, or lower issue prices to compensate for higher risks. This chapter focuses on the implication of the bail-in regime on the liability mix of banks. The introduction of the bail-in caused an increase in the overall cost of funding but also a reallocation among financing instruments according to the risk premium imposed by the bail-in hierarchy.

2.2 The Bank Liability Mix: The Role of Deposits

There are three main categories of liabilities for a commercial bank: deposits, equity, and other liabilities such as bonds. Bank depositors represent the traditional funding source of banks. Bank deposits are very important also from a financial stability point of view. Bank runs have been associated with depositors' behavior and may lead to systemic crises. Bank runs occur when many banks' customers withdraw their deposits simultaneously for fear of a potential bank crisis. Bank run episodes recurred regularly in history: for instance, during the great depression in the United States (1929). More recently, the British bank "Northern Rock" experienced a bank run in 2007, which was eventually resolved through the acquisition of the bank by the government. However, the most recent case occurred in Greece in 2015, when the threat of Greece leaving the Euro and the European Union caused panic among the depositors that run to their banks to withdraw their money. The run was mitigated by closing some banks temporarily and by imposing limits on withdrawals.

An effective deposit insurance scheme is needed to prevent bank runs (Diamond & Dybvig, 1983). Essentially, deposit insurance guarantees that banks' depositors will be honored in the event of a bank failure. In the European Union, deposit insurance is currently granted by the national governments. Still, there is the plan to implement a pan-European Deposit Guarantee Scheme as the 3rd pillar of the EBU.[1] Currently, deposits in the EU are generally guaranteed up to a limit of 100,000 euros per deposit account per bank in case of a bank default. Let's consider an example, in which a depositor, Thomas, has 130,000 euro deposited in "Bank Alpha." If Bank Alpha fails and the bail-in regime is applied, first equity and then the outstanding bonds should be used to cover the losses. However, if there are still bank losses to be covered, depositors may be called to cover the remaining part. In this case, however, Thomas will bear the losses only up to a limit of 30,000 euro because the other 100,000 are insured. This insurance has the purpose of safeguarding the depositors' savings and preventing panic among the depositors in case of a bank crisis.

Depositors must be adequately informed on the coverage provided by the deposit insurance available in their country to make sure that deposit insurance prevents a bank run. They should be well aware that even during a bank crisis, their deposits will never be lost. Unfortunately, there is evidence in the literature that investors lack this perfect information, at least in some cases (Safakli & Guryay, 2007). Furthermore, Goedde-Menke et al. (2014) showed that depositors were well informed on deposit insurance at the peak of the Global Financial Crisis and raised their deposits. However, in the aftermath of the crisis, as soon as the perception of risks in the system declined, depositors strongly reduced their deposit even below pre-crisis values, in turn increasing the probability of bank run.

On the other hand, deposit insurance leads to moral hazard and risky behaviors, excessive bank risk-taking, and a general lack of market discipline on the depositors' part. Depositors are more likely to select less carefully the bank where to deposit their savings, thus giving banks lower

[1] For details see Chapter 1.

incentives to assess the granting of new loans and monitoring them carefully. Imai (2006) tested the market discipline of Japanese depositors after an upper bound limit for deposit insurance was established in Japan. He found evidence in favor of greater market discipline once the unlimited deposit insurance was removed.

For what concerns depositors' reaction specifically at bail-in events, the main reference is Brown et al. (2017), analyzing the event related to the bail-in involving Bank of Cyprus. The authors find that households withdrew their deposits and reallocated them in cash holdings, Carboni and Scardozzi (2021) agree finding a decrease in depositors trust after the announcement of the bail-in.

This chapter extends this analysis by testing if the liability mix of Euro Area Banks changed after the revision of the banking resolution policy in the European Banking Union. The bail-in makes bail-inable liabilities more expensive according to the bail-in hierarchy and therefore increases incentives for banks to rely more on cheaper sources of funding (in particular deposits that are the most protected instrument by the bail-in provision). While bank deposits tend to be a stable source of funding during non-crisis periods, a higher reliance on deposits increases banks' asset-liability mismatching, and expose banks' to higher liquidity risk, threatening their financial soundness during periods of financial stress.

The greater reliance on deposits by banks could raise financial stability concerns in the current environment, characterized by the COVID-19 pandemic and the consequent economic crisis due to lockdowns and other restrictive measures aimed at limiting the spreading of the virus. Enterprises facing liquidity shortages, as a consequence of the impossibility to operate in the context of a health emergency, might withdraw the money deposited in the banks. A massive withdrawal could constitute a significant liquidity risk for banks as they may not be able to repay all the depositors.

2.3 Euro Area Banks' Sources of Funding

What are the consequences on the bank's liability structure when implicit public guarantees are removed (or reduced)? The new European resolution regulation provides an ideal case since the regulation changed from a bailout to a bail-in framework, and the creditors' protection hierarchy was publicly announced.

The bail-in hierarchy leads to a different increase in risk for bonds and deposits as bonds have lower legal protection under the scope of the bail-in. Consequently, investors are likely to ask for higher returns for bonds vis-à-vis for deposits. This increase in the cost of bonds may incentivize banks to rebalance their liability structure by reducing the weight of more expensive financing instruments. Customer deposits are the most legally protected liabilities because of their position at the very bottom of the bail-in hierarchy and they are insured by the Deposit Guarantee Scheme and the national insurance to a limit of 100,000 euro. The other sources of funding, subordinated and senior bonds, are less shielded from the scope of the bail-in as bondholders are the second category of investors to bear bank losses after equity holders. The launch of the bail-in might have caused a shift from more expensive and less legally protected instruments, as subordinated and senior bonds, to less expensive and more legally protected instruments, such as deposits.

The literature has extensively studied the liability mix of banks especially in conjunction with crisis periods. On the one hand, funding sources other than deposits (core liabilities) exposed banks to greater vulnerability to crises (Hahm et al., 2013). Vazquez and Federico (2015) pointed out that banks with high liquidity risk and leverage have a greater probability of failing during a crisis. At the same time, banks' greater reliance on deposits is costly due to higher asset-liability mismatching and the pricing of possible bank runs. Also, higher levels of deposits result in banks holding "unproductive" reserves (Diamond & Dybvig, 1983).

We represent the Euro Area liability mix using accounting data from the Fitch Connect database from 2009 to 2017. Figure 2.1 shows the liability mix before and after the launch of the bail-in.

The figure shows trends in funding sources for Euro Area banks distinguishing according to the level of legal protection granted by the bail-in mechanism. We can observe how the liability mix changed during the period analyzed. Euro Area banks increased the share of the less expensive sources of funding (customer deposits) that benefit from stronger legal protection according to the BRRD while decreasing the share of those sources of funding that became riskier under the bail-in provisions. Table 2.1 provides more specific information on the growth rates of such funding sources in the period analyzed.

The greatest positive growth rate pertains to the less expensive source of funding. Customer deposits grew at a rate of 9.24% in 2015, when the BRRD became effective. For what concerns the more expensive

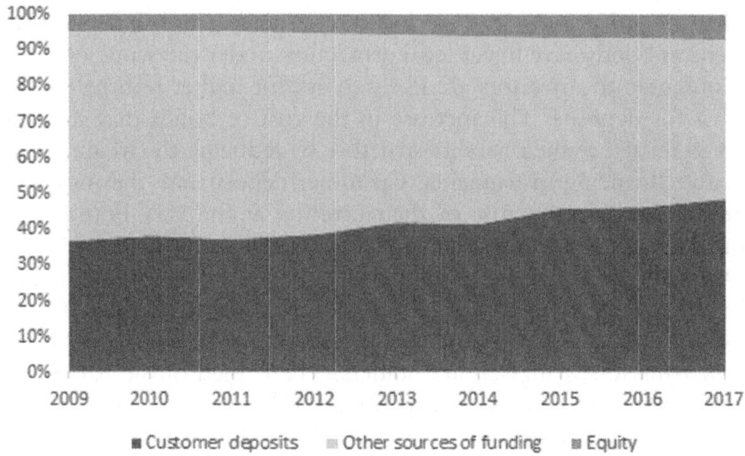

Fig. 2.1 Euro Area banks' sources of funding (*Note* The figure shows the Euro Area banks' liabilities mix from 2009 to 2017. The figure shows that during this period there was a progressive increase in customer deposits and in equity—possibly due to the concurrent increase in capital requirements—while other sources of funding [like bonds] decreased as a fraction of the Euro Area banks' liabilities. *Source* Authors' own using Fitch data)

Table 2.1 Sources of funding growth rate

Year	*Customer deposits (%)*	*Other sources of funding (%)*	*Equity (%)*
2010	3.32	−2.36	3.29
2011	−2.04	1.50	−1.65
2012	3.74	−2.96	6.79
2013	8.90	−7.24	12.34
2014	−0.79	0.20	3.91
2015	9.24	−8.20	7.15
2016	1.67	−1.95	2.66
2017	4.92	−5.57	5.22
Average	3.62	−3.32	4.96

Note The table reports the growth rates of customer deposits, other sources of funding, and equity of Euro Area Bank. The growth rate is calculated as (source of funding in t − source of funding in t − 1)/ (source of funding in t − 1)

Source Authors' own using Fitch data

funding sources, labeled as "other sources of funding" in the table, these registered the greatest negative growth rate in the same year, −8.20%. While the table provides only suggestive evidence, it points to a clear shift in financing sources for the Euro Area banking sector, possibly due to the implementation of the different pillars of the Banking Union and the increases in regulatory requirements: on average, the cheapest source of funding (e.g., deposits) increased annually in the Euro Area by 3.62%, while other sources of funding, more expensive due to the bail-in hierarchy, decreased by 3.32%. At the same time, equity increased on average by 4.96% on an annual basis due to the more stringent capital requirements implemented by regulation.

The change in the composition for Euro Area banks' funding sources has great relevance for the banking system's financial stability. The greater reliance on short-term source of funding, such as deposits, exposes the banks to maturity mismatch and hinders financial stability via an increase in the liquidity risk, which could materialize during times of financial distress or in the events of large exogenous shocks.

2.4 The Role of the Bank Risk in the Liability Mix Changes

Policymakers foster financial stability also by improving the market discipline. Market discipline refers to the capacity of holders of banks' liabilities (depositors, bondholders, and equity holders) to recognize and monitor the risks undertaken by banks and, consequently, to manage their investments accordingly. To enforce market discipline, the market participants should be aware and correctly informed on the banks' risks; moreover, they should have adequate incentives to monitor them. These incentives may not be very high as long as the bailout remains an option since depositors and bondholders will continue relying on the implicit guarantee provided by the government on their investments. The introduction of the bail-in aims at ruling out such implicit guarantees, enhancing incentives for market participants to monitor the bank risk-taking. Within this framework, it is important to evaluate the role of the bank risk to assess better whether there are improvements in the market discipline.

If the bail-in effectively improved the market discipline, we would expect riskier banks to experience greater changes in their funding composition due to the market discipline enforced by market participants that would ask for greater returns to fund riskier banks. Consequently, riskier banks should face a greater cost of funding and seek to increase reliance on relatively cheaper financing sources. Essentially the bail-in should make the investors better aware of the different levels of risk associated with the EU banks.

A measure of the risk taken by banks is the level of impaired loans. The measure impaired loans is disclosed every year with the bank's financial statement, allowing market participants to be aware and informed on the level of risk undertaken and realized by the bank. Those banks with a greater share of loan impairment should face difficulties in raising their funds or, at least, they should face a greater cost of funding especially through those financing instruments that are riskier according to the bail-in hierarchy. Using the abovementioned financial data, Fig. 2.2 shows evidence of this shift. Panel A displays the liability mix for Euro Area riskier banks, while Panel B shows the same for the safest banks. The first are those banks with a share of loan impairment over total assets above the 75th percentile. At the same time, the latter are those Euro Area banks with the lowest share of loan impairment over total assets (below the 25th percentile).

In Panel A of Fig. 2.2, we observe that the relative shares of bonds and customer deposits reverse for riskier banks, starting from 2014. Riskier

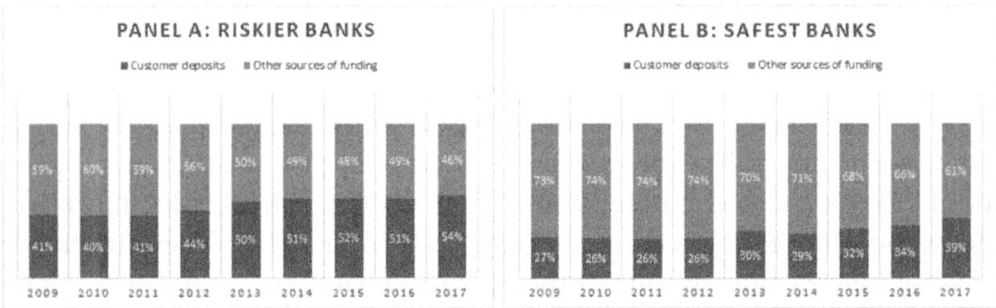

Fig. 2.2 Sources of funding according to the bank risk (*Note* The figure shows the Euro Area banks sources of funding according to the riskiness of the bank. Specifically, Panel A plots the liability mix of the riskier banks, while Panel B refers to the safest banks. The measure used to identify riskier and safest banks is the share of impaired loans over total assets. The variable has been divided into quartiles, and the banks with a share of loan impairment over total assets in the 4th quartile belong to the "riskier" banks (Panel A), while the banks with a share in the 1st quartile belong to the "safest" group (Panel B). *Source* Authors' own using Fitch data)

banks shifted their financing strategy from a greater reliance on other funding sources, such as bonds, to a liability mix mostly composed of customer deposits. In 2017, one year after the bail-in became effective, riskier banks funded themselves to a greater extent through cheaper liabilities (customer deposits, 54%) and less with expensive funding sources like bonds (46%). We can observe in Panel B that the safest banks maintain the same liability mix, with a greater reliance on expensive sources of funding relative to customer deposits; this implies that the riskier banks mainly drive the overall results highlighted in Fig. 2.1. The market discipline, enhanced by introducing the bail-in provision, determined a radical change in the liability mix for riskier banks, leading them to prefer cheaper liabilities and customer deposits as a financing source. In comparison, safer banks maintained the previous liability mix characterized by a greater bond component.

2.5 The Role of the Bank Size in the Liability Mix Changes

The bail-in tool generated substantial concerns among the investors (equity holders, bondholders, depositors), particularly due to the uncertainty on whether the tool would indeed be implemented in cases of bank resolution. The Too-Big-To-Fail (TBTF, thereinafter) issue has been often mentioned in this context. The failure of large banks is much more dangerous for financial stability. The banking system is an interconnected network where the largest banks are critical nodes, and it has been argued that the bail-in of such critical banks would not be implemented for fear of detrimental systemic consequences. The lawmakers intervened on this issue by clarifying that the bail-in discipline would be mandatory after the 1st January 2016, implying that no exceptions would have to be expected.

The concept of TBTF has been present in the banking literature for a long time, and indeed, it has justified public intervention in the resolution of banks. More recently, issues related to the systemic impact of large banks came to the surface, particularly with the episode of the collapse of Lehman Brothers, the 4th largest North-American bank, in 2007. The bankruptcy of this bank, which resulted from the subprime loans crisis in the United States, had enormous consequences on the global financial sector and eventually triggered the Global Financial Crisis (GFC). Many Euro Area banks were also highly exposed to subprime assets, and several banks in Europe were bailed out using State aids. Using financial support, governments would rescue systemically significant banks, as the bankruptcy of such financial giants could hinder financial stability worldwide. Market participants began, therefore, to feel sure of their investments in large banks and, as a consequence, moral hazard and greater recklessness in bank risk-taking became widespread phenomena. However, the sovereign debt crises that affected European sovereigns soon provided an indubitable example of the damages caused by State aid provided to large banks to restore their financial conditions and their operability. Levels of sovereign debt increased substantially in several European crises because of the liquidity injected into the banking system. The sovereign debt crises in the EU started in 2008 with the collapse of Iceland's banking system and peaked between 2010 and 2012, leaving national governments unable to further bailout banks on the verge of bankruptcy. After some cases of bail-in, implemented by the European governments well before the new resolution regime entered into force,[2] market participants realised that the issue was no longer a matter of TBTF institutions but rather a matter of banks Too-Big-To-Save (TBTS, there in after).

The current analysis assumes that if the investors believe that the new bail-in framework will not apply in concrete cases of large banks' default, they would not ask for greater yields on risky instruments issued by larger banks (TBTF case). Alternatively, if investors believe that governments cannot bailout large banks since these are TBTS, they would ask for greater yields on risky instruments issued by large and riskier banks (TBTS case).

Figure 2.3 plots the same shares as Fig. 2.2, but the two panels refer specifically to larger banks—with total assets greater than 30 billion euro[3] and smaller banks—with total assets lower than 30 billion euro.

Panel A displays the case of large banks, clearly showing that the trend in their liability mix confirms the previous findings, i.e., the increase in reliance on deposit funding. In Panel B, we instead observe the opposite trend for the liability mix of smaller banks. These decreased their

[2] Case of Banco Popular described in Chapter 4.

[3] 30 billion euro asset volume is the threshold of one of the requirements currently used by the European Central Bank to classify a bank as a "Systemically Important Bank" and, consequently, one of the requirements for the bank to be supervised by the Single Supervision Mechanism.

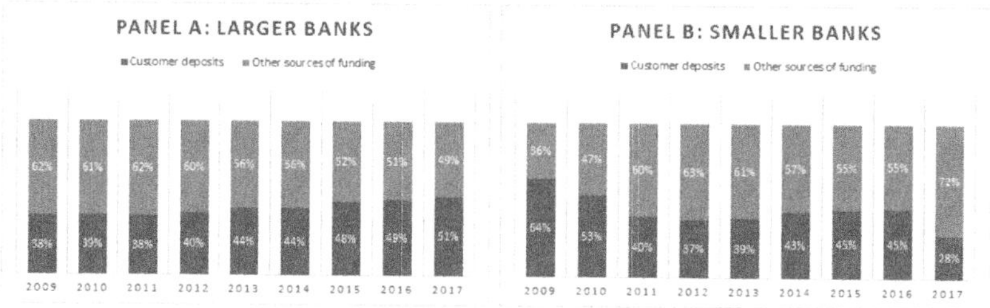

Fig. 2.3 Sources of funding according to the bank size (*Note* The figure shows the Euro Area banks sources of funding according to banks' size. Specifically, Panel A plots the liability mix of the large banks, while Panel B refers to the small banks. The threshold for significant banks used by the ECB identifies large and small banks; the former are those with total assets greater or equal than 30 billion euros (Panel A), while the latter have total assets lower than 30 billion euros (Panel B). *Source* Authors' own using Fitch data)

reliance on customer deposits in favor of other sources of funding. This suggests that the TBTF as a concept is no longer considered a possibility by market participants who deem the bail-in regulation credible enough. Moreover, the question of TBTF reverted into a TBTS and the largest banks adjusted their liability mix more than the smaller banks, as also outlined by Demirguc-Kunt and Huzinga (2013). After establishing the bail-in mechanism, market participants might think that governments are unable to afford the bailout of large banks. Therefore, they preferred to buy riskier instruments from smaller banks.

2.6 Empirical Evidence

Inspired by the descriptive analysis that we presented in the previous sections, we provide some robust evidence of a change in the liability mix of Euro Area banks due to the establishment of the bail-in. We implement a regression model that captures the effect on the bank funding structure after the announcement of the new resolution mechanism. The sample consists of banks in the Euro Area that are subject to the new bail-in regulation. To consider anticipation behaviors (Fiordelisi et al., 2017), we consider the treatment period (e.g., the period of the regulation effect) starting with the first announcement of the bail-in regulation, which occurred in June 2012; hence, the treatment period is 2013–2017.

We include in the sample only Euro Area banks because for most European countries outside the Euro Area, the application of the BRRD was postponed, and banks in those countries might not have reacted to the announcement of the directive. As such, European banks in non-Euro Area countries have been discarded from the sample.

To assess the policy impact as the bail-in was announced, we exploit a "before and after" regression model to capture the effect of the announcement of the bail-in on bank liabilities.

$$Y_{i,t} = \alpha + \beta \text{ Time}_t + \text{Total Asset}_{i,t} + \frac{\text{Loan Impairment}}{\text{Total Asset}_{i,t}} + \sigma_c + \varepsilon_{i,t} \quad (2.1)$$

Υ is the bank liability ratio, defined either as customer deposits or other sources of funding over total assets. Time is a treatment variable that equals 1 from the year after the announcement of the bail-in (2013) onward and a value of 0 before the bail-in was announced. The coefficient of Time can assess the effect of the launch of the bail-in on the liability mix. The other variables included in the model account for the size and the risks undertaken by the bank, variables whose relations with the outcome were outlined in the previous section. In particular, these variables are the asset size (Total Assets) and the level of risk captured by the ratio of loan impairment over total assets. Country fixed effects are also included in the model (σ), and the errors are clustered by bank. The results of this regression model are reported in Table 2.2.

The β coefficient of the dummy Time, which equals 1 for Euro Area banks between 2013 and 2017 and 0 for Euro Area banks before 2013, is the one of main interest to our analysis. This coefficient provides information about the effect of the introduction of the new bail-in framework. A positive β coefficient suggests an increase in the dependent variable, while a negative slope signals a decrease in the dependent variable. Table 2.2 reports the results using as dependent variables the ratio of customer deposits (column 1) and other funding sources (column 2), respectively. Both coefficients of the treatment variable Time are statistically significant at the 1% level. The coefficient is positive for the customer deposits ratio, while it is negative for the other sources of funding used as response variables. As shown in column (1) and (2) of Table 2.2, Euro Area banks rebalanced their liabilities: they increased (+4.3%) the quota of total assets financed by deposits after the announcement of the bail-in, compared to

Table 2.2 Before and after regression model results

Variables	*Customer deposits ratio*	*Other Sources of funding ratio*
Time	0.043***	−0.073***
	(0.004)	(0.009)
Total asset	−0.001***	0.001***
	(0.000)	(0.000)
Loan impairment ratio	0.306	2.459**
	(0.230)	(0.965)
Observations	15,000	15,000
R-squared	0.355	0.471
Fixed effect	Issuer Country	Issuer Country
Error clustered	Bank	Bank

Note The table reports the results of model (1)
*,**,*** represent the statistical significance at 1%, 5% and 10%, respectively
Source Authors' own using Fitch data

the previous period, and reduced (−7.3%) the quota of assets financed by other sources of funding, namely bonds. The bail-in hierarchy stated that bondholders are less shielded than depositors in case of default. Therefore, other sources of funding like bonds became riskier than deposits and their holders asked for a higher return, making the instruments more expensive than customer deposits. The results in Table 2.2 support the previous graphical analysis: Euro Area banks changed their liability mix after the announcement of the bail-in by relying more on deposits, the cheapest source of funding after the bail-in resolution mechanism was established.

2.7 Conclusion

The new European resolution regime marked the shift from a bailout perspective to a bail-in regime and represented a milestone event for banking regulation. As an exogenous shock, the approval of the bail-in regime led the banks to rebalance their sources of funding via a cost-based restructuring in their funding strategy. The bail-in determined a greater risk for some securities, according to the hierarchy clarified in the BRRD. The incremental risk outlined by the bail-in tool to banks' investors induced a greater cost of funding for Euro Area banks. To face the increase in the cost of funding, banks rebalanced their liability mix.

The chapter analyzes the liability mix in the Euro Area countries after the 2007–2009 GFC and during the creation of the European Banking Union. The descriptive evidence and the regression analysis captured the difference in the liability mix before and after the new resolution regime in the EU. Essentially, the relative costs of different sources of funding changed due to the bail-in hierarchy. Deposits are at the bottom of the bail-in hierarchy, and the government partly insures them. Therefore, the introduction of the bail-in regime resulted in a relatively low-risk premium for deposits, making customer deposits the cheapest financing source for banks. At the same time, instead, introducing the bail-in imposed a greater risk premium on bonds due to their position as subordinated to deposits in the coverage of bank losses.

Figure 2.1 plots the weights of customer deposits and other sources of funding in terms of total assets. The figure shows an increase in the weight of deposits over bank size as Euro Area banks relied more on deposits and decreased their share of other funding sources. After the bail-in hierarchy was disclosed, market participants asked for a greater return in order to hold less protected securities. At the same time, depositors remained at the bottom of the bail-in hierarchy and benefited from the explicit guarantee by governments (3rd pillar of EBU on deposit insurance scheme). This brought Euro Area banks to rebalance their liability mix according to the relative increase in the cost of funding.

This is an important result, especially for policymakers. Relying on deposits can have costly consequences in terms of financial stability because of larger asset-liability mismatches, increased risks of bank runs, and higher levels of unproductive reserves (Diamond & Dybvig, 1983). The implication on liquidity risk is of great importance: The increase of deposit funding increases the liquidity risk. Being exposed to liquidity risk could constitute for Euro Area banks an element of potential vulnerability in stress periods like the environment induced by the COVID-19 pandemic. To face the several lockdowns imposed by national governments, enterprises may withdraw their highly liquid deposits at short notice, making those banks that rely excessively on them unable to pay back their depositors.

Furthermore, this chapter highlights that the investors' are ready to penalize riskier banks by asking for higher compensation. This result supports the improvement of market discipline, a desirable outcome for those policymakers pursuing financial stability.

Finally, the problem of TBTF institutions reverted into a TBTS one. The chapter shows that the larger banks decreased their reliance on other funding sources compared to deposits, while smaller banks did not change their liability mix. An economic interpretation of this is that the bail-in was deemed credible for TBTF banks. Investors strongly believed that the governments would not have been able to bailout bigger banks after the implementation of the bail-in framework.

References

Brown, M., Evangelou, I., & Stix, H. (2017). Banking crises, bail-ins and money holdings. *Central Bank of Cyprus Working Paper.*

Carboni, M., & Scardozzi G. (2021). La fiducia dei depositanti nel nuovo strumento di risoluzione bancaria. *Rivista Bancaria Minerva Bancaria, 3*, 75–106.

Crespi, F., & Mascia, D. (2018). Bank funding strategies. *Palgrave Macmillan Studies in Banking and Financial Institutions.*

Cutura, J. (2018). Debt holder monitoring and implicit guarantees: Did the BRRD improve market discipline? *SAFE Working Paper Series.*

Demirguc-Kunt, A., & Huzinga, H. (2013). Are banks too big to fail or too big to be save? International evidence from equity prices and CDS spreads. *Journal of Banking and Finance, 36*, 2145–2156.

Diamond, D. W., & Dybvig, P. H. (1983). Bank runs deposit insurance, and liquidity. *Journal of Political Economy, 91*, 401–409.

Fiordelisi, F., Ricci, O., & Stentella Lopes, F. S. (2017). The unintended consequences of the launch of the single supervisory mechanism in Europe. *Journal of Financial and Quantitative Analysis, 52*, 2809–2836.

Giuliana, R. (2019). Impact of bail-in on banks bond yields and market discipline. *Working paper available at SSRN.*

Goedde-Menke, M., Langer, T., & Pfingsten, A. (2014). Impact of the financial crisis on bank run risk-danger of the days after. *Journal of Banking and Finance, 40*, 522–533.

Hahm, J., Shin, H. S., & Shin, K. (2013). Noncore bank liabilities and financial vulnerability. *Journal of Monet, Credit and Banking, 45*, 3–36.

Imai, M. (2006). Market discipline and deposit insurance reform in Japan. *Journal of Financial Stability, 15*, 264–281.

Safakli, O., & Guryay, E. (2007) A research on designing an effective deposit insurance scheme for TRNC with particular emphasis on public awareness. *International Research Journal of Finance and Economics, 7.*

Shafer, A., Schnabel, I., & di Mauro, B. W. (2016). Bail-in expectations for European banks: Actions speak louder than words. *ESRB Working Paper Series.*

Vazquez, F., & Federico, P. (2015). Bank funding structures and risk: Evidence from the global financial crisis. *Journal of Banking and Finance, 61*, 1–14.

CHAPTER 3

Risk Allocation and Bond Mis-selling After the Bail-in Directive

Abstract This chapter analyzes the holding of bail-inable securities. During 2012–2013, several cases of mis-selling occurred in European countries as banks sold risky bonds to retail investors as "safe assets." The chapter shows how bond holdings across different types of investors has evolved in recent times. Before the approval of the new resolution regime, the mis-selling was a widespread financial phenomenon, especially in Southern Euro Area countries. However, allocation of bonds across sectors changed after the launch of the bail-in resolution mechanism; households sold their bank bonds to other, more sophisticated, financial intermediaries. This suggests that the new European Resolution mechanism was effective in reducing the mis-selling of bank bonds.

Keywords Bond holdings · Bond · Bail-in · Portfolio allocation · Mis-selling

3.1 Introduction

Mis-selling is a financial phenomenon that repeatedly occurred over at least the last two decades. Mis-selling refers to those cases in which complex securities like bank bonds are sold to investors lacking

A. M. Maddaloni and G. Scardozzi, *The New Bail-In Legislation*, Palgrave Macmillan Studies in Banking and Financial Institutions, https://doi.org/10.1007/978-3-030-87560-2_3

adequate levels of financial sophistication and, therefore, unable to evaluate correctly the risk inherent to these investments. Financially unsophisticated investors typically belong to the retail sector, mainly composed of households, many of whom have low levels of financial literacy. They are generally looking for a safe investment for their savings. Over the past years, there have been several cases in Europe in which complex securities were sold to households not fully aware of the risks involved, notwithstanding measures to increase consumer protection, like the most recent implementation of the Markets in Financial Instruments Directive (MIFID) directive [2014]. In many of these cases, banks misguided their investors (Colaert and Incalza, 2018). For example, the Italian bank Banca Etruria, in 2013 advertised its subordinated bonds as a safe investment to its customers. The case of Banca Etruria is well known because when the bank fell in trouble, many bondholders, that due to the mis-selling of these securities were in large part households rather than institutional investors, lost their life savings.[1]

Cases of mis-selling occur when complex securities are sold to investors that are not able of discerning the risk inherent to these instruments due to a lack of financial literacy. Financial literacy, or better the lack thereof, is the main driver of mis-selling behavior. Retail investors do not have the ability or the necessary information to accurately estimate the risks implicit in bank bonds, especially subordinated securities. In recent years, the need to improve financial literacy has been largely recognized by regulators, and ad hoc regulations were conceived to safeguard consumers. At the same time, there seems to be still room to be covered to ensure the enforcement of these regulations. The main regulation for consumer protection against mis-selling is the MIFID, which has been approved in [2014]. The directive implies that certain securities are not compatible

[1] These episodes had huge and at times tragic repercussions as a pensioner committed suicide after losing the savings of a lifetime (Reuters, 10 December 2015, https://www.reuters.com/article/uk-italy-banks-rescue-death/pensioners-death-turns-up-heat-in-row-over-italy-bank-rescue-idUKKBN0TT1JV20151210). Banca Popolare di Vicenza, another Italian bank, engaged in similar misconduct as it loaned larger amounts to borrowers so that they could invest part of the loan in bonds issued by the same bank (Reuters, 29 September 2016, https://www.reuters.com/article/italy-banks-popvicenza-probe/italy-bank-popolare-vicenza-probed-over-loans-for-shares-scheme-idUSL5N11V28H20150929).

with low levels of risk and therefore are not recommended for households. However, the directive does not forbid the sale of such securities, and mis-selling can still occur.

At the same time, many unsophisticated investors relied on the implicit government guarantee in case of a bank failure. They did not account for the possibility to lose their money in case of bank default. The transition from a bailout resolution regime, implemented at the country level, to the bail-in resolution mechanism meant that the resolution of failing banks would be managed without using taxpayers' money, but rather enforcing the write-down of banks liabilities' to restore the bank's capital. The Bank Recovery and Resolution Directive (BRRD) clarifies that the risk increases for bank securities. The definition of the bail-in hierarchy should have made investors better aware of the level of risk implicit in the different types of securities. In this sense, the bail-in should have improved the market discipline inducing investors to be alert and monitor of banks risk-taking behavior. Improving the market discipline is one of the main objectives of the new resolution framework. Inadequate levels of financial literacy and sophistication could, however, hinder the achievement of such a result.

In this chapter, we analyze whether the new regulatory regime for banks' resolution has been effective in preventing—at least to a certain extent—the occurrence of episodes of mis-selling by improving the market discipline and promoting a better allocation of bank bonds. The analysis conducted exploits a unique dataset on security holdings in Europe, extracted from the European Central Bank's proprietary database Security Holding Statistics (SHS). This database stores quarterly data on holdings for worldwide securities by investors resident in the Euro Area from 2009 onward. The SHS database collects information on the holder (holder type, holder country, amount held), on the security (type of security, price, yield), and the issuer's country.

3.2 Literature Review

Within the literature on financial literacy, several papers have shown that retail investors are not able to properly evaluate both the stability of a bank and the risks implicit in its liabilities (Lusardi et al., 2014). Conversely, professional and institutional investors (such as insurances, mutual and pension funds) are the ideal target for complex financial products: They have the capability, professional skills, and available data to accurately evaluate the risk-return combination of complex financial products (de Dreu & Bikker, 2012).

A number of event studies are conducted around the dates of the regulation and/or around some resolution cases. They analyze the effect on bond yields by looking at investors' reactions to changes in banking regulation and, more specifically, to changes in the bank resolution mechanism (Crespi & Mascia, 2018; Cutura, 2018; Giuliana, 2019); stock returns (Fiordelisi et al., 2020) and CDS (Pancotto et al., 2019).

In this chapter, we analyze investors' reactions in terms of bank bond holdings due to the change in the European resolution regime from a bailout to a bail-in resolution tool. We also discuss whether the new banking regulation mitigated the mis-selling phenomenon, which is particularly relevant issue for policymakers.

The detailed features of SHS data allow us to analyze whether the allocation of bonds issued by Euro Area banks has been affected by the launch of the new resolution tool. We would expect a reduction of bank bond holdings by retail investors, who have limited capacity to assess the riskiness of financial instruments issued by banks. In particular, a desirable result from a policy point of view would be a reduction in retail investors' holdings of subordinated debt once investors realize the removal of the implicit guarantee—no bailout possible. On the contrary, professional and institutional investors are an ideal target for those securities, and therefore should increase their holdings of subordinated debt.

3.3 Graphical Analysis

This section reports the allocation of bonds held in the Euro Area using the SHS database. This database stores quarterly data on holdings for worldwide securities held by different types of Euro Area resident investors from 2009 onward.[2] Information on the holding refers to the holder sector, holder country, and the amount held in nominal and market value for each specific security. Moreover, the database reports the issuer type (bank, non-financial corporations, government) and the issuer country.

Within the SHS dataset, we select bonds issued by Euro Area banks from the first quarter of 2010 to the end of 2019, avoiding any

[2] SHS database before 2013 wear collected as pilot.

Table 3.1 Holder sector classification

Holder sector	*Group*
Non-financial corporations	NFCs
Deposit-taking institutions except for Central Banks	Banks
Money Market Funds (MMF)	Other Financial
Insurance Corporations	Intermediaries (OFIs)
Pension funds	
Non-MMF Investment funds	
Financial vehicle corporations	
Households	Households
Non-profit institutions serving households	
Government	Excluded

Note The table reports the rule of classification of the holder sectors available in the SHS database. The 4 groups are formed according to the level of financial sophistication
Source Author's production using SHS information

confounding effects due to the COVID-19 pandemic. We clustered holder sectors into four categories according to their level of financial sophistication: Non-financial corporations (NFCs), Banks (deposit-taking institutions except for Central Banks), Households (households and Non-profit institutions serving households), and Other Financial Intermediaries (OFIs Money Market Funds, Insurance Corporations, Pension funds, Non-Money Market Funds Investment funds and financial vehicle corporations). Table 3.1 summarizes the holder sector categories.

The analysis in this chapter keeps separated the banks' sector from the OFIs' sector, and consider the latter as the sector including the most financially sophisticated institutions. Banks and OFIs are both financially sophisticated investors; however, we argue that the OFIs are better equipped to fully assess the risk implicit to subordinated securities as some of the financial intermediaries included in this group target high-risk investment. In contrast, banks are mainly oriented toward consumers, being deposit-taking corporations.

Figure 3.1 displays the allocation of bonds[3] across the main investor groups over time, namely the quota of instruments held by each sector,

[3] We exclude from the sample covered bonds because they are classified as suitable also for households' financial profile being out of the scope of the bail-in ex art 44(2) of

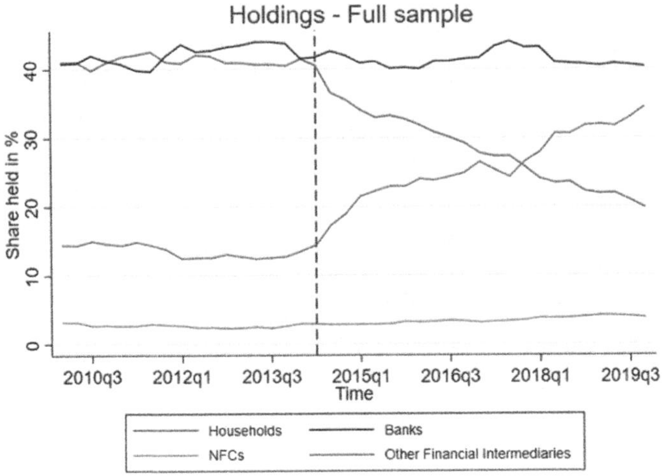

Fig. 3.1 Holdings of bank bonds (*Note* The figure shows the share held by each investor group. The share is calculated as the nominal amount held by households for all bonds in a given quarter over the total amount held by all types of investors in the same quarter. *Source* Author's own using SHS dataset)

calculated as the nominal amount of a given security held by each category of holder sector over the total amount held by all holder sectors. It is evident from the figure that, in 2010, households held the greatest share of bonds issued by banks together with the banking sector (about 40% each). Financial intermediaries other than banks (the investor category with the highest financial sophistication), detained only 15% of the bonds issued by banks in the same year. Finally, NFCs held a small portion of such bonds (around 5%). Allocation was relatively stable over time until the second quarter of 2014 (vertical dashed line in Fig. 3.1), the quarter in which the BRRD and, specifically, the bail-in provision was approved (April 2014). From the BRRD approval onward, the household sector drastically reduced its holdings of bonds issued by banks, from the previous 40% to around 20% by the end of 2019. The figure shows that households sold the bank bonds to the OFIs. OFIs bought bank bonds, increasing their holdings from 15 to 35%. This descriptive

the BRRD directive according to which covered deposits, secured liabilities, and liabilities with a remaining maturity of less than seven days are not bail-inable.

evidence suggests a reduction of mis-selling after the BRRD and the bail-in regulation came into force. By the end of the sample (last quarter of 2019), bank bonds were held for the largest part by the most financially sophisticated investors (banks and OFIs), better equipped to understand the risk and the complexity of these securities.

However, the increase in holdings of bank bonds from OFIs and other banks is also a reason for concern since it may increase contagion risks. Cross-selling, namely banks holding bonds issued by other banks, is a serious concern within the new resolution framework. In case of a bank failure, the bail-in tool should be applied, and the bonds written down to cover bank losses may amplify the risk of contagion.

It is also interesting to analyze in which country the BRRD was more effective in mitigating mis-selling. Figure 3.2 report the graphical analysis accounting for the issuer country. We combine issuer countries into three groups: Northern, Central, and Southern countries of the Euro Area. Northern countries are Estonia, Finland, Ireland, Latvia, Lithuania, and the Netherlands. Central countries are Austria, Belgium, Germany, Luxembourg, Slovakia, Slovenia, and France. Southern Countries are Cyprus, Greece, Italy, Malta, Portugal, and Spain.

This figure plots the share of bonds held by each investor group and issued by banks located in one of the three geographic regions within the Euro Area. Panel C (Southern countries) presents the trend most similar to Fig. 3.1: Households held the greatest portion of bank bonds in 2010 and moved from holding more than 50% to around 25% by the end of the sample; they sold those bonds to OFIs which increased their share from 10% to more than 30%. The growth rate of the share held by households became negative since the second quarter of 2014 when the bail-in was approved, while the growth rate of the share held by OFIs became positive around the same period.

In Panel A, we can observe that the decreasing trend in households' share and the increasing trend in OFIs' share set off years before the establishment of the bail-in mechanism. Since the beginning of 2011, households sold bonds issued by Northern banks to OFIs, suggesting that factors other than the new banks' resolution tool determined this trend. Finally, in Panel B (Central countries), we can observe that the holdings of banks' bonds by households were initially much lower; only a slight reduction in the share of bonds held by households in favor of OFIs' holdings occurred in the second quarter of 2014.

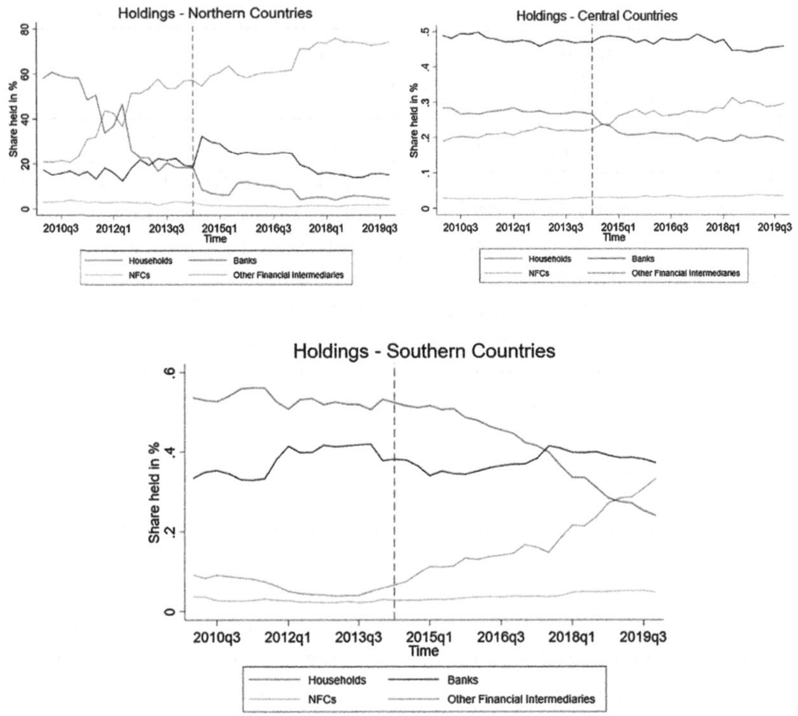

Fig. 3.2 Holdings of bank bonds according to issuer geographic region. *Panel A*: Holdings by Northern countries; *Panel B*: Holdings by Central countries; *Panel C*: Holdings by Southern countries (*Note* The figure shows the share held by each investor group in three subsamples related to the geographic region of the Euro Area: Panel A includes the bonds issued by Estonia, Finland, Ireland, Latvia, Lithuania, and the Netherlands (Northern countries); Panel B includes the bonds issued by Austria, Belgium, Germany, Luxembourg, Slovakia, Slovenia, and France (Central countries). Finally, Panel C includes the bonds issued by Cyprus, Greece, Italy, Malta, Portugal, and Spain (Southern countries). The share is calculated as the nominal amount held by households for all bonds in a given quarter over the total amount held by all types of investors in the same quarter. *Source* Author's own using SHS data)

Overall, the evidence described in Panel C suggests that the mis-selling was a phenomenon more frequent for banks residing in Southern countries and that the new resolution regime may have mitigated it by improving the allocation of those bonds considered riskier according to the BRRD.

Starting from this result, we zoomed in on the group of Southern Euro Area countries to analyze the trend for holding bonds issued by banks residing in each of these countries. Figure 3.3 describes the dynamics of bond holdings across holder sectors for Italian issuers, one of the countries in which problems of mis-selling have been more acute.

This figure is very similar to Fig. 3.1. This means that mis-selling was a phenomenon particularly widespread among Italian banks. The new resolution regime effectively mitigated this type of misconduct, at least for what concerns banks' bonds held by households. However, in Italy, the reallocation of sectoral portfolios resulted in a significant increase in banks' bonds held by other banks and by NFCs. This led to an allocation in which banks resident in the Euro Area are the main holders of

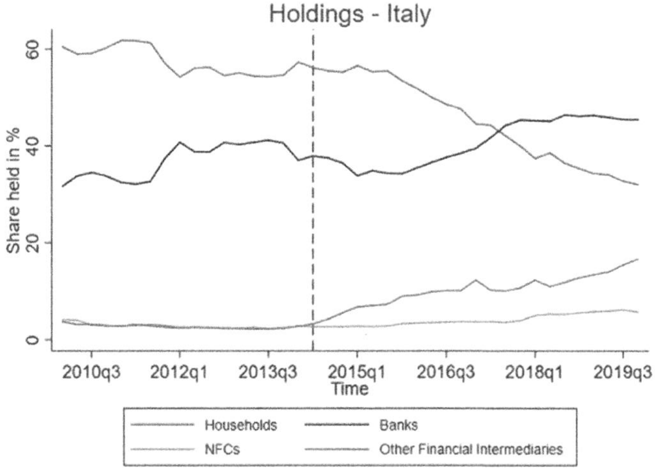

Fig. 3.3 Holdings of bonds issued by Italian banks (*Note* The figure shows the share held by each investor group. The share is calculated as the nominal amount held by households for bonds issued by Italian banks in a given quarter over the total amount held by all types of investors in the same quarter. *Source* Author's own using SHS data)

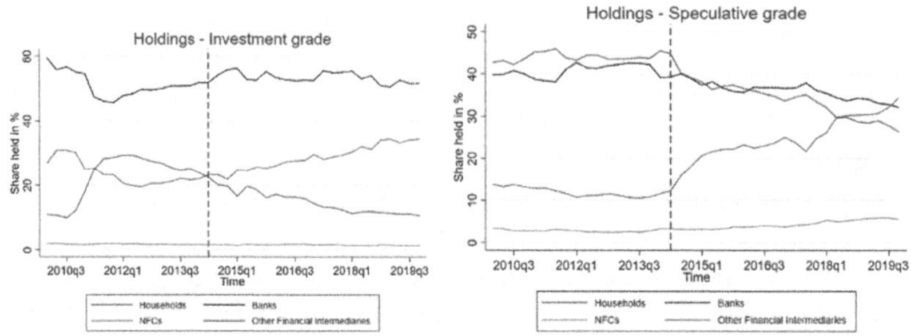

Fig. 3.4 Holdings of bonds according to their ratings (*Note* The figure shows the share held by each investor group. Panel A shows the subsample of the "Investment-grade" bonds (with ratings in the range AAA–BBB). Panel B shows the subsample of the "Speculative-grade" bonds (with ratings below BBB). The share is calculated as the nominal amount held by households in a given quarter over the total amount held by all investors in the same quarter. *Source* Author's own using SHS data)

Italian bank bonds at the end of 2019 (around 50%), amplifying the risk of contagion throughout the banking system resulting from the bail-in resolution mechanism.

Overall, the graphical analysis confirms that the approval of the bail-in provision was able to mitigate episodes of misconduct linked to the mis-selling, triggering a process of reallocation of bank bonds holdings: nowadays, banks and OFIs hold around 80% of the bank bonds. A substantially smaller quota is held by households, around 17% (Fig. 3.1).

Until now, we spoke about mis-selling in all those cases when households held a large share of bank bonds. To ascertain that the cause of this holdings' allocation is mis-selling, we extend the analysis across holder sectors and classes of rating. The MIFID does not recommend bank bonds to households, especially those bonds that have a low rating assigned by rating agencies. Therefore, we aggregated the ratings into two classes: "Investment grade" and "Speculative grade." The first category includes the bonds with the best rating (from AAA to BBB), the second category includes bonds with a rating below BBB.[4] Figure 3.4

[4] In case more than one rating agency assigns a rating to a specific bond with we took the median of the ratings available. Bonds without rating are not included in the figure.

reports the trends in the holdings of these two categories of securities.

The graphs confirm the misallocation of the speculative-grade bank bonds before the revision of the resolution regime in Europe, as Panel B clearly shows that the holders of these very risky securities were mainly households. In 2010, the household sector held 42% of the speculative-grade bonds issued by Euro Area banks, while OFIs—the most financially sophisticated investors—held 15% of such instruments. Later on, after the bail-in approval, the households' holdings of speculative bank bonds were reduced and the holdings by the OFIs increased. A similar decline in risky security holdings can be observed for the banking sector (from 40 to 32%), suggesting that banks aimed at improving their asset quality.

According to the data shown in Panel A, we can observe that the mis-selling was not an issue concerning investment grades bonds at the beginning of 2010, even though a peak in households holdings was registered at the beginning of 2011, followed by a decrease of such holdings one year later.

From the preliminary evidence showed above, the new resolution regime has determined a reallocation of the bonds issued by Euro Area banks across holding sectors. The re-balancing mainly involved transferring bank bonds from the household sector to the most financially sophisticated investors (OFIs). This may have improved market discipline and reduced instances of mis-selling.

3.4 Empirical Analysis

The previous analysis shows how the holdings of bonds issued by Euro Area banks changed for the different investors' categories in the last few years. This section aims to assess through an empirical analysis whether the new resolution tool, introduced with the BRRD, improved market discipline by aligning risk-taking behaviors with investors financial literacy, and reduced the scope for mis-selling.

To test whether the new bail-in regime succeeded in re-aligning investors' risk-taking with their level of financial literacy, the following regression model, based on a before-after approach, is implemented:

$$\begin{aligned} Y_{i,t} = \alpha + \beta_1 \text{ Time}_t + \beta_2 \text{ HomeBias}_{i,t} + \beta_3 \text{ ResidualMaturity}_{i,t} \\ + \beta_4 \text{ Yield}_{i,t} + \beta_5 \text{ Rating}_{i,t} + \sigma_c + \varepsilon_{i,t} \end{aligned} \tag{3.1}$$

Table 3.2 List of variables

Variable name	*Description*
Time	Dummy equal to 1 from the approval of the BRRD in the second quarter of 2014 until the end of the sample, 0 otherwise
HomeBias	The percentage of the bond held domestically in a given quarter
ResidualMaturity	Years remaining until maturity
Yield	The quarterly yield of the bond
Rating	Dummy equal to 1 for investment-grade bonds. The rating is the average of the ratings assigned within a given quarter when more ratings are available for the same bond

Note Variable names and the relative description
Source Authors' own using SHS information

where i is the bond identifier (ISIN number) and t is the time-quarter of observation. The dependent variable $\Upsilon_{i,t}$ is the ratio of the nominal value of bonds held by one type of investors—households, NFCs, banks, or OFIs—over the total nominal amount held by all investor types for security i at the end of the quarter t.

The model includes the variable Time, a dummy for the quarter of the treatment taking the value of 1 from the second quarter of 2014—when the BRRD was approved—and 0 otherwise. This dummy variable can capture any reduction or increase in the holdings of a given holder sector after the approval of BRRD and the introduction of the bail-in provision. The regression also includes a set of control variables: HomeBias is the share of the bond i held domestically, namely the percentage of the security held in the country of issuance; ResidualMaturity is a bond sensitive variable, included to account for differences in the holdings due to the remaining time to maturity; finally, Yield and Rating proxy the bond riskiness.

The model includes country of issuance fixed effects. The list of the variables used in the regression with the relative descriptions is reported in Table 3.2.

3.5 Results

The regression model is estimated for each holder category: households, banks, NFCs, and OFIs. Table 3.3 reports the results of the estimation of model (3.1).

Table 3.3 Regression model results

Variables	*(1)* *Households*	*(2)* *Banks*	*(3)* *NFCs*	*(4)* *OFIs*
Time	−0.012***	0.001***	0.001***	0.011***
	(0.000)	(0.000)	(0.000)	(0.001)
HomeBias	0.280***	0.988***	1.000***	0.949***
	(0.001)	(0.000)	(0.000)	(0.001)
ResidualMaturity	−0.001***	−0.000***	0.000***	0.003***
	(0.000)	(0.000)	(0.000)	(0.000)
Yield	0.000**	0.000	0.000	−0.000
	(0.000)	(0.000)	(0.000)	(0.000)
Rating	−0.131***	0.006***	0.000*	0.019***
	(0.001)	(0.000)	(0.000)	(0.001)
Constant	0.697***	0.010***	0.000***	0.036***
	(0.000)	(0.000)	(0.000)	(0.000)
Observations	1,202,779	671,489	556,451	237,413
R-squared	0.328	0.989	0.998	0.912
FE	Issuer country	Issuer country	Issuer country	Issuer country

Note The table reports the results of model 3.1 run for the four holder categories: households (column 1), banks (column 2), Non-Financial Corporation (NFCs, column 3), and Other Financial Intermediaries (OFIs, column 4)
Standard errors in parentheses
*** $p < 0.01$, ** $p < 0.05$, * $p < 0.1$
Source Authors' production using SHS data

The model assesses the effect of the BRRD approval on bank bond allocation. The regression sample includes observations from the first quarter of 2010 to the last quarter of 2019.

Time is the variable of interest; its coefficient captures whether and to which extent the investor category (displayed on each column of Table 3.3) increased or decreased its holdings of bonds issued by Euro Area banks after the BRRD and the bail-in came into effect.

Time is highly statistically significant for all investor categories, meaning that after the approval of the new resolution tool, the bank bond allocation changed.

For what concerns households' reaction, the empirical analysis confirms the evidence provided by the graphical representation: Households decreased their holdings of bank bonds after the approval of BRRD. However, the magnitude of the coefficient is smaller than what was suggested by the previous charts. According to the regression results, households decreased their quota of bank bonds only by 1.2% (column 1, Time). Although the magnitude may be smaller due to the control variables included in the regression model, the coefficient of Time remains highly statistically significant, confirming a reaction by households to the establishment of the new resolution regime.

For what concerns the other investor categories, all of them increased their holdings of bank bonds after the BRRD was approved (column 2–4). However, we conclude that banks and NFCs increased their share of holdings by a very small amount (around 0.1%). In comparison, the most financially sophisticated holder sector increased their holdings the most: Other financial intermediaries increased by 1.1% the quota of bank bonds held (column 4, Time). This result confirms that the most important reallocation across sectors resulted from households to OFIs.

Among the other control variables, HomeBias deserves further attention. HomeBias describes the share of a bond held domestically within a given investor category. The variable is highly statistically significant and positive for all investor categories: It indicates that on average, the bonds are mainly held domestically.

The variables Yield and Rating are proxies for the bond risk. Among the two, Rating is the variable considered more by the investors when changing their allocation of bank bonds. Yield is almost always statistically not different from zero and negligible, while the Rating is almost always statistically significant. Looking at the Rating coefficient, we can observe that only households decreased their holdings of bank bonds when the bonds were rated as investment-grade securities while the other sectors, instead, increased them. NFCs did not change allocation according to the rating, and the Rating coefficient in column 3 is weakly statistically significant (at 10% level) and its magnitude negligible (around 0%). This draws our attention to the previous graphical analysis: Households sold more of their bonds with a better rating, and this is probably linked to the peak we observed in Fig. 3.4 at the beginning of 2011.

3.6 Conclusion

After the global financial crisis, the European Banking Union harmonized the banking resolution mechanism for the EU. After the sovereign debt crisis, bailouts were no longer a viable alternative. At the same time, market discipline had to be restored to enhance financial stability. The analysis reported in this chapter assesses whether these goals were achieved with the launch of the bail-in resolution tool and whether the new resolution regime also mitigated concerns for mis-selling.

The descriptive analysis shows that before the new resolution regulation mis-selling was a widespread financial phenomenon, especially in Southern Euro Area countries. Households held mainly speculative-grade bonds, identifying a marked misallocation of such securities from 2010 to 2014. After the approval of the bail-in mechanism, households sold their bank bonds to other more sophisticated financial intermediaries.

The subsequent empirical analysis confirms the results. Households reduced their holdings of bonds issued by banks, while other (specialized) financial intermediaries—such as money market funds and financial vehicle corporations—increased them. Therefore, we can assume that households sold the bonds issued by Euro Area banks to the most financially sophisticated sector after the BRRD and the bail-in were approved. The other two holder categories, NFCs and banks, did not exhibit, instead, a substantial change in their bond holdings.

In general, evidence suggests that the resolution regime reform mitigated the mis-selling phenomenon: retail sectors (households) reduced their holdings of bank bonds issued by Euro Area banks, while more financially sophisticated institutions increased their holdings. At the end of 2019, before the COVID-19 pandemic, bank bonds were mainly held by the two most financially sophisticated sectors (banks and OFIs). At the same time, this suggests that cross-selling—banks holding bonds issued by other banks—may be an issue of concern for the Euro Area banking system, as contagion risks increased and may realize in case of a bank failure and implementation of the bail-in regime.

References

Colaert, V., & Incalza, T. (2018). Mis-selling of financial products: Compensation of investors in Belgium. European Parliament June 2018.

Crespi, F., & Mascia, D. (2018). Bank funding strategies. Palgrave Macmillan Studies in Banking and Financial Institutions.

Cutura, J. (2018). Debt holder monitoring and implicit guarantees: Did the BRRD improve market discipline? *SAFE Working Paper Series n.232.*

de Dreu, J. A., & Bikker, J. (2012). Investor sophistication and risk taking. *Journal of Banking and Finance, 36*, 2145–2156.

Fiordelisi, F., Minnucci, F., Previati, D., & Ricci, O. (2020). Bail-in regulation and stock market reaction. *Economic Letters, 186.*

Giuliana, R. (2019). Impact of bail-in on banks bond yields and market discipline. https://dx.doi.org/10.2139/ssrn.2935259

Lusardi, A., Mitchell, O. S., & Curto, V. (2014). Financial literacy and financial sophistication in the older population. *Journal of Pension Economics and Finance, 13*, 347–366.

Pancotto, L., Gwilyim, O., & Williams, J. (2019). The European bank recovery and resolution directive: A market assessment. *Journal of Financial Stability, 44*.

CHAPTER 4

Bond Allocation After Bank Resolution Cases

Abstract Investors may not react to the approval of the regulation (as analyzed by the previous chapter) and may not realize the inherent risk in certain instruments (e.g. bail-inable bonds) until banks are actually experiencing distress. In 2017, several distressed banks that had issued bail-inable debt were actually resolved. Case studies of the major resolution events are discussed in this chapter (e.g. Banco Popular, the Italian "Venetian Banks," and Monte dei Paschi di Siena). Evidence is provided on the implications of the implementation of the bail-in; results suggest that the banking sector in aggregate increased the nominal amount held of bail-inable bonds issued by riskier banks relative to safer banks (possibly impairing financial stability by increasing the risk of contagion in case of a bank failure), whereas other financial institutions decreased their holdings.

Keywords Bond holdings · Bank distress · Banco Popular · Banche Venete · Monte dei Paschi di Siena

4.1 Introduction

The bail-in tool became effective on January 1, 2016. Therefore, starting 2016, all cases of bank in distress should have been managed within

A. M. Maddaloni and G. Scardozzi, *The New Bail-In Legislation*, Palgrave Macmillan Studies in Banking and Financial Institutions,
https://doi.org/10.1007/978-3-030-87560-2_4

the Bank Recovery And Resolution Directive (BRRD) framework, with the bail-in tool implemented. In 2017, several European banks fell into financial distress, presenting the first opportunity to implement the new resolution rules and in turn to assess the effects arising from the application of the bail-in tool.

In this chapter, we study the changes in bond allocation following the events of bank crises in mid-2017. While Chapter 3 assesses the improvements in market discipline after the new directive for resolution was approved, this chapter's analysis relies on the events of bank distress in mid-2017. The analysis conducted in this chapter is two-fold. First, we aim at evaluating the credibility of the bail-in as to whether supervisory and resolution authorities were credible in enforcing the bail-in regime after it came into force. Second, we assess whether actual bank distress cases further[1] improved the allocation of bank bonds along the lines proposed by Shafer et al. (2016), who compared CDS reactions at the events corresponding to the different regulation phases (e.g. first announcement, publication of the draft, formal approval) with CDS reactions to the actual resolution of a set of European banks. Focusing on four major bank distress cases (Banco Popular, Veneto Banca, Banca Popolare di Vicenza, and Monte dei Paschi di Siena), we study the reactions of bondholders to verify the impact on bonds' allocation and the credibility of the new resolution regime.

The credibility of the enforcement of the bail-in tool is of great relevance. Philippon and Salord (2017) state that to enhance market discipline effectively, investors must expect to bear the losses in case of a bank failure. The credibility issue has been discussed in the literature. Several studies analyze credibility through an event study of abnormal stock returns around normative or real events (Fiordelisi et al., 2020), on CDS premia (Pancotto et al., 2019), and on bond yields (Crespi & Mascia, 2018). Shafer et al. (2016) compare market reactions to the announcement and approval of the regulation with the reactions to the actual implementation of the bail-in tool, finding that the latter caused stronger reactions than the announcement or the approval of the BRRD did. However, there is no analysis assessing the norm's credibility by looking at the volumes rather than at market prices. This chapter aims to assess the credibility of the new resolution tool by analyzing whether

[1] In the third chapter, we have argued that the approval of the bail-in regulation in the second quarter of 2014 caused an improvement of bank bond allocation.

the retail sector (e.g. households) sold bank bonds after the distress of the four banks occurred.

The issue of Too-Big-To-Fail (TBTF) is also of great relevance in this context. Securities issued by the biggest banks, the Globally Systemically Important Banks (G-SIBs), should have a stronger market reaction than securities issued by other banks because the really large banks were benefiting the most from implicit government guarantees. O'Hara and Shaw (1990) find that TBTF banks experience a positive average abnormal return on the announcement date, while other banks have negative abnormal returns. However, bailouts and state aids undermined the bail-in tool's credibility among investors. Some studies emphasize the trade-offs implicit in the different resolution regimes. Avgouleas and Goodhart (2015) argue that a bailout may be justified because it avoids contagion effects, systemic crises, and capital flights. Keister (2016) finds that imposing the bail-in may lead intermediaries to invest in too-liquid assets, thereby lowering aggregate welfare.

In the previous chapter, we provided a preliminary analysis of the bond allocation among the four categories of investors (households, non-financial corporations, banks, and other financial intermediaries). This chapter focuses on the changes in bond allocation after the four cases of bank distress that occurred in Spain and Italy. The aim is to analyze whether the enactment of the regulation, rather than its approval, changed the allocation of bonds that became bail-inable on January 1, 2016.

4.2 The Events

In 2017, four cases of bank distress occurred in Europe. They were the cases of Banco Popular in Spain, Veneto Banca, Banca Popolare di Vicenza, and Monte dei Paschi di Siena in Italy. These bank distress events were the first to occur after the bail-in became effective. Therefore, they represented the first opportunity to apply the new resolution regime and analyze its effects. In the following sections, we describe in details the course of events resulting in the banks' failures.

4.2.1 Banco Popular

Banco Popular was a bank located in Spain, founded in 1926. The bank grew rapidly: since the early 2000s, its total assets quadrupled, and its profitability doubled (Santos, 2017), becoming in 2017 the sixth-largest bank in Spain operating domestically and internationally. This rapid growth was fostered through an aggressive investment policy. However, the several mergers with the *cajas*—to support weak institutions—resulted in Banco Popular having a huge amount of non-performing loans. Banco Popular's capital position was weak in 2017. These problems generated a lack of confidence among investors, and Banco Popular started to face liquidity shortages. The European Banking Authority assigned negative results to Banco Popular in the 2016 stress test, asking for the issuance of new shares to improve the bank's capitalization. After several shareholders meetings, negative media coverage, higher expected losses (in the first quarter of 2017, the losses amounted to 3.5 billion euro), the downgrading in April 2017 and, finally, the Spain Minister of Economy's declaration that the bank would not receive state support, the stock price went down by more than 10% and the bank experienced a large deposit outflow, estimated around 30 billion euros (Banco Santander Confident, 2017). The ECB declared Banco Popular as "failing or likely to fail" on June 6, 2017, due to a "significant deterioration of its liquidity situation."

The Single Resolution Board (SRB) adopted a resolution scheme on June 7, 2017, and this was approved the same day by the European Commission. The resolution had to be implemented according to the BRRD at the European level in the public's interest.

The SRB required the application of two tools: the sale of the assets and the bail-in. Therefore, the SRB wrote down the CET1, AT1 capital, and the T2 capital was converted into new shares; these newly issued shares were sold to Banco Santander for the symbolic price of 1 euro, and the management of Banco Popular was replaced. The role of Banco Santander was to provide liquidity. The resolution did not involve at all the Single Resolution Fund and the national deposit guarantee fund. The resolution of Banco Popular constituted the first example of the application of the new European resolution regime.

4.2.2 Veneto Banca and Banca Popolare di Vicenza

Veneto Banca and Banca Popolare di Vicenza were located in Italy. Veneto Banca had been in trouble since 2013, while the Single Supervisory Mechanism found similarly critical issues in the Banca Popolare di Vicenza at the beginning of 2015. The two banks were liable for serious episodes of misconduct as they granted loans to their shareholders and undermined their capital position. This determined a loss of trust from the investors of these two banks. The mistrust translated into liquidity shortages. To address the liquidity crisis affecting these two banks, they issued in February 2017 the first 6.5 billion euros of bonds covered by the government guarantee; one month later, an additional 3.6 billion euros of guaranteed securities were issued for a second tranche. Veneto Banca and Banca Popolare di Vicenza had to provide the authorities with a restructuring plan; as they could not find private resources to fund this plan, on March 17, 2017, the two banks asked for precautionary recapitalization to the Italian Ministry of Finance. On June 23, 2017, Veneto Banca and Banca Popolare di Vicenza were declared "failing or likely to fail." The decision to not provide precautionary recapitalization to the two banks arrived two days afterwards, after an in-depth discussion among the Bank of Italy, the European Central Bank, and the European Commission, which eventually resulted in the liquidation of the two banks.

The assets and liabilities of the two banks were transferred to Intesa San Paolo, the largest bank in Italy. The SRB assessed that the failure of the two banks did not harm "public interest" because they operated predominantly at regional level. Therefore, the new resolution regime did not apply in these cases, and the two banks were liquidated according to national insolvency proceedings.

Senior bondholders and depositors were transferred to Intesa San Paolo without suffering any loss, while subordinated bondholders and equity holders were part of the liquidation to cover the losses. Under art. 32 of the BRRD, before any form of state aid is granted, the losses should be covered first by equity holders and then by subordinated bondholders.

The distress of the two banks occurred in the second quarter of 2017 (when the BRRD was already in force). However, the resolution was implemented according to national insolvency proceedings because the defaults were of no public interest and involved partial public assistance. A second argument for the public assistance granted to the creditors of the two banks is linked to the fact that many investors bought these banks' bonds before the approval of BRRD (mid-2014). Subsequently, the Italian government argued with the European authorities that only bonds issued after the BRRD's approval (January 1, 2015) should be considered bail-inable.[2]

4.2.3 Monte dei Paschi di Siena

On December 31, 2016, Monte dei Paschi di Siena (MPS) was Italy's third-largest lender and the world's oldest bank.

MPS had been posting losses since 2014, especially due to a large amount of non-performing loans. In 2015, the ratio of non-performing loans over total loans was about 22%, much higher than the Italian average (10.8%), which was already much higher than the European one. The European Central Bank requested, many times, to reduce such amount of non-performing loans. In 2016, the bank stress test assessed that MPS was the only bank whose CET1 ratio was forecast as negative in the 2018 adverse scenario; if the adverse scenario was to materialize, the bank would have suffered an 8.8 billion euro capital shortfall.

In July 2016, MPS announced a restructuring plan for 5 billion euro to recapitalize the bank. Equity holders and part of subordinated bondholders were written down or converted into equity. However, MPS failed to raise enough funding on the market to meet its capital requirements and, on December 23, 2016, turned to the government asking for state aid.

Finally, on July 4, 2017, the European Commission approved the state aid for 5.4 billion euro for MPS (bailout), just a few days before the Italian government granted public assistance to Veneto Banca and Banca Popolare di Vicenza. In the case of Monte dei Paschi, the state aid was deemed compliant to the BRRD under article 32(4) on precautionary recapitalization because MPS financial troubles entailed the potential for a severe financial crisis. Moreover, equity holders and subordinated bondholders covered part of the losses up to 4.3 billion euro during 2016.

4.3 Empirical Analysis

The following analysis aims to understand whether the allocation of bail-inable securities across holding sectors was affected when the bail-in was implemented effectively. This section analyzes to what extent the

[2] https://www.bancaditalia.it/media/notizie/2017/crisi-banche-venete/index.html.

resolution tool was perceived as credible by each type of investor eventually affecting bank bond allocation in the Euro Area. This contributes to the existing literature analyzing the new resolution tool's credibility. While other papers look at the overall market reactions, we look at the bank bond allocation, assessing whether the distress of banks may incentivize the retail sector to sell bank bonds to more sophisticated financial intermediaries.

The results deserve the attention of those policymakers that: (a) aim at enhancing the credibility of the bail-in tool by the market participants; (b) aim at safeguarding the retail investors from buying risky securities; (c) try to prevent banks from buying bonds issued by other banks due to the contagion risk; (d) strive to improve the market discipline among investors. The analysis compares changes in the holdings of bonds issued by risky banks with the allocation of bonds issued by the "safest" banks. After cases of bank distress, we expect the investors to realize that investments in risky banks could be written down in case of a bank failure. Hence, non-speculative investors (such as households) should decrease their holdings of these bonds vis-à-vis holdings of bonds issued by safer banks. This is true only if investors recognize the concrete possibility that the bail-in is applied after witnessing the resolution of banks in distress.

For this analysis, we implement a difference-in-difference technique. To define a treated and a control group, we use two different identification strategies to divide the banks into two groups based on their riskiness. The first identification is based on market data and uses daily yields of bail-inable bonds for each bank, extrapolated from the IBoxx database. The second identification strategy relies on information from the banks' financial statements from the Orbis BankFocus database to obtain information on size and impaired loans. In both cases, the idea is to compare holdings of bonds issued by banks with a risk profile similar to the risk carried by defaulted banks with the holdings of bonds issued by safer banks.

The analysis takes advantage of three different databases, two of which contain ECB proprietary data. The main dataset used to analyze the bonds holdings is the SHS database, collecting the amount held of each bond by each holder sector. The IBoxx database is used to implement the first propensity-score matching. This database collects daily data, aggregated at the bank level, on the yield of subordinated and senior bonds for the major banks of the Euro Area. For each event, we run a propensity-score matching with 20 neighbors on the decile of the yields in the same month but one year before the event. The matched units are the treated banks. Among the unmatched observations, we select as controls the banks with, on average, the lowest level of bonds yield (the "safest" banks). The matching has been implemented cross-country. The number of observations in the sample, according to time and investor category, is displayed in Table 4.1.

As Table 4.1 shows, the analysis is limited to the number of quarters included. To identify the investors' reaction to the bank distress cases that occurred in the second quarter of 2017, and to avoid confounding effects due to the bail-in approval (first quarter of 2016), we include in the analysis only two quarters before and two quarters after the event, dropping the quarter of the event. The investor categories are the same as discussed in the previous chapter.

One may argue that investors do not look at the market data (e.g. yield) when identifying the riskier banks and, consequently, changing the amount held of the bonds issued by those banks. Investors might, however, look at the banks' financial statements. To implement the second matching, we collect the financial statement data from Orbis BankFocus. Both the size and the level of impaired loans could be good proxies of the riskiness of a bank. More specifically, we argue that size is a risk factor because of the TBTF concern. The biggest banks had, in fact, the government implicit guarantees before the introduction of the new resolution regime. Consequently, this analysis entails a propensity-score matching on the level of total assets one year before the event. Among the matched units, the treated group includes half of the banks with the highest level of impaired loans ratio (impaired loans over total assets). The control group includes the remaining banks (the ones with the lowest

Table 4.1 Sample composition (units matched according to market data)

Quarter	*No.*	*Investor category*	*No.*
2016q4	537	Households	250
2017q1	535	Banks	455
2017q3	443	Non-financial corporations	169
2017q4	423	Other financial Intermediaries	1064
Total	1938	Total	1938

Note The table reports the number of observations in the sample obtained by implementing a propensity-score matching based on the aggregate yield. The table reports the distribution across quarters and across investor categories

Source Authors' calculation using SHS data

Table 4.2 Sample composition (units matched according to financial information)

Quarter	*No.*	*Investor category*	*No.*
2016q4	339	Households	433
2017q1	343	Banks	464
2017q3	358	Non-financial corporations	217
2017q4	352	Other financial Intermediaries	278
Total	1392	Total	1392

Note The table reports the number of observations of the sample obtained by implementing a propensity-score matching based on size and impairment loans ratio. The table reports the distribution across quarters and investor categories
Source Authors' calculations using SHS data

level of impaired loans ratio). While the matching based on bond yields is conducted at the cross-country level, in the second matching we look for similar banks within the country where the default events took place (e.g. Spain for Banco Popular, and Italy for the other events). This matching takes into account the home bias behavior by market participants. The number of observations in the sample, according to time and investor category, is displayed in Table 4.2.

Once treated and control groups are defined, we estimate a standard difference-in-difference model.[3] The regression model implemented is the following one:

$$Y_{i,t} = \alpha + \beta_1 \text{ Time}_t + \beta_2 \text{ Treatment}_{i,t} + \beta_3 \text{ PriceGrowth}_{i,t} + \delta_i + +\varepsilon_{i,t} \tag{4.1}$$

Here, the dependent variable, Υ, is the natural logarithm of the nominal amount of bonds held by each investor category.[4] Then, the model includes the Treatment variable, which is the variable that labels

[3] To enhance the use of this policy evaluation method, we test the parallel trends hypothesis using a F-Fisher test for the treated and control groups by measuring the joint probability that the Average Treatment Effect moves around 0 in the pre-treated period. For both models (yield and financial statement matching), the parallel trend assumption is verified.

[4] Contrary to the analysis conducted in Chapter 3, because of the application of the difference-in-difference policy evaluation tool, we test the holdings using the nominal amount held instead of the quota held (nominal amount held by one type of investors over the total amount held by all investors) to avoid unbalanced results.

the product between a dummy identifying the two groups (equal to 1 for treated banks and 0 for banks in the control group) with the Time dummy referred to the period (equal to 1 from the third quarter of 2017, the quarter after Banco Popular, Banche Venete, and Monte dei Paschi di Siena fell in distress, and 0 before).[5] Due to the nominal nature of the dependent variable (nominal amount held), we need to control for the change in bond prices. Therefore, the model includes PriceGrowth computed as $(\text{Price}_t - \text{Price}_{t-1})/\text{Price}_{t-1}$.

The sample includes the period from the fourth quarter of 2016 to the fourth quarter of 2017. The quarter of the event (second quarter of 2017) was dropped from the sample. As a result, the final sample includes the two quarters before the treatment. We include only long-term uncovered bonds (with original maturity longer than 10 years) for sample uniformity. Finally, δ_i represents the security fixed effects.

4.4 Results

Table 4.3 shows the results of the regression model, implementing the matching on yield. The resolution of these banks caused a reallocation of bank bonds across sectors. More specifically, non-financial corporations decreased their nominal holdings of bonds issued by riskier banks relative to bonds issued by the safest banks—the coefficient of Treatment in column 3 is negative and statistically significant (10%). Conversely, the banking sector increased the amount held of bonds issued by riskier banks relative to the safest banks—the coefficient of Treatment in column 1 is positive and significant (1%). The analysis suggests that the distress of four banks in Europe induced an increase in the amount of bail-inable bonds held by the banking sector. These results imply that financial stability is hindered by the moral hazard endemic to the banking sector. Moreover, they suggest low credibility of the bail-in enforcement within the banking sector.

To address concerns related to, especially retail investors that may change their allocation of bonds according to the level of risk captured by the banks' financial statements rather than the yields from the market, we conduct the same analysis using the matching on size and impaired loans ratio.

[5] We do not include the variable w due to the presence of security fixed effect

Table 4.3 Allocation of bail-inable bonds after the bank distress cases in mid-2017 (matching on yield)

Variables	*Households*	*Banks*	*NFCs*	*OFIs*
Time	−0.320**	−0.087**	−0.171	−0.056
	(0.162)	(0.036)	(0.187)	(0.053)
Treatment	−0.341	0.099***	−0.866*	−0.033
	(0.305)	(0.034)	(0.447)	(0.057)
Price Growth	3.743**	0.890	0.998	0.002
	(1.544)	(1.402)	(2.174)	(0.077)
Constant	15.99***	16.37***	14.79***	15.19***
	(0.074)	(0.016)	(0.110)	(0.015)
Observations	250	455	169	1064
R-squared	0.919	0.976	0.777	0.978
FE	Security	Security	Security	Security

Note The table reports the results of a difference-in-difference regression model. The dependent variable is the natural logarithm of the nominal amount held by households (column 1), banks (column 2), non-financial corporations (column 3), and other financial intermediaries (column 4). The sample includes long-term bonds with maturity in 2019–2020. The sample includes observations from the fourth quarter of 2016 until the fourth quarter of 2017, excluding the quarter of the event (second quarter of 2017). The Time dummy takes values equal to 1 from the third quarter of 2017 (the quarter immediately after the event). The treatment group is composed by bail-inable long-term bonds, issued by banks as risky as the failing banks; the control group includes bail-inable long-term bonds issued by the safest banks. The definition of risky and safe is based on the implementation of a propensity-score matching on the level of the aggregated yield. Treatment is the coefficient of interest. It represents the interaction of the Time dummy with the dummy identifying the groups: it captures the joint effect of a risky bank after the bank distress cases
*,**,*** represent the level of significance, 10%, 5%, and 1%, respectively
Source Authors' calculations using SHS data

Table 4.4 shows the results where the treated and control groups are formed by matching the observations by size and impaired loans within countries. The Treatment variable is statistically significant only for the most financially sophisticated sector, the other financial intermediaries (column 4). The negative coefficient suggests that the most financially sophisticated sector reduced the nominal amount held of bonds issued by large and risky banks (with a size and a level of impaired loans ratio comparable to Veneto Banca, Banca Popolare di Vicenza, Monte dei Paschi di Siena, and Banco Popular) relative to the safest banks in the same country (Italy or Spain).

Overall, the analysis results suggest that the bail-in application is credible for most of the financial sector, where intermediaries reallocated their

Table 4.4 Allocation of bail-inable bonds after the bank distress cases in mid-2017 (matching on financial statement data)

Variables	*Households*	*Banks*	*NFCs*	*OFIs*
Time	−0.085***	0.050	0.041	0.298**
	(0.012)	(0.036)	(0.042)	(0.119)
Treatment	−0.038	0.067	−0.078	−0.382***
	(0.039)	(0.065)	(0.066)	(0.123)
Price Growth	0.283*	−0.074	1.028	−0.778
	(0.164)	(0.410)	(0.712)	(0.997)
Constant	14.67***	16.61***	12.80***	14.17***
	(0.012)	(0.019)	(0.026)	(0.059)
Observations	433	464	217	278
R-squared	0.997	0.988	0.991	0.972
FE	Security	Security	Security	Security

Note The table reports the results of the difference-in difference regression model. The dependent variable is the natural logarithm of the nominal amount held by households (column 1), banks (column 2), non-financial corporations (column 3), and other financial intermediaries (column 4). The sample includes long-term bonds with maturity in 2019–2020. The sample includes observations from the fourth quarter of 2016 until the fourth quarter of 2017, dropping the quarter of the event (second quarter of 2017). The Time dummy takes values equal to 1 from the third quarter of 2017 (the quarter immediately after the event). The treatment group is composed by bail-inable long-term bonds, issued by banks defined as risky as the failing banks; the control group includes bail-inable long-term bonds issued by the safest banks. The definition of risky and safe is based on the implementation of a propensity-score matching on size and non-performing loans. Among the matched observations, half of the banks with the greatest non-performing loans ratio formed the treated group and the remaining half formed the control group. Treatment is the coefficient of interest. It represents the interaction of the Time dummy with the dummy indicating the groups: it captures the joint effect of a risky bank after the bank distress cases

*,**,*** represent the level of significance, 10%, 5%, and 1%, respectively

Source Authors' calculations using SHS data

bond holdings toward safer institutions. This is likely to reduce, rather than increase, market discipline: other financial intermediaries are generally better positioned to assess and manage the risk of instruments issued by riskier banks. At the same time, the analysis implies that the issue of mis-selling may not be solved: after the resolution of the banks within the new framework, the retail sector (households) did not reallocate their financial portfolio significantly away from risky banks' bonds.

4.5 Conclusion

The effectiveness of regulators' commitment hinges on the perceived credibility of the market. The credibility of the bail-in tool has been discussed at length by academics and policymakers around the implementation of the new resolution regime. More specifically, some studies provided evidence that the market reacted at the bail-in events by analyzing CDS premia and abnormal stock returns. At the same time, conceptual frameworks pointed out that the state aid provided to the banking system—in different forms—reduced the credibility of bail-in applications in the future. This chapter analyzes this issue by looking at the reallocation of banks' bonds across different sectors in correspondence with four events of banks' distress. In mid-2017, three Italian banks (Veneto Banca, Banca Popolare di Vicenza, and Monte dei Paschi di Siena) and a Spanish bank (Banco Popular) fell in distress, and resolution procedures were undertaken. For Veneto Banca and Banco Popolare di Vicenza, a hybrid form of bail-in/bailout was applied, while the Italian government injected liquidity (in the form of capital) to rescue Monte dei Paschi di Siena. In Banco Popular, a pure bail-in resolution procedure was implemented by writing down equity holders and subordinated bondholders. We use these events to implement an empirical difference-in-difference analysis to verify whether the bond allocation across sectors changed after these events. We classify the banks in two groups according to their riskiness, and we use two different identification strategies to form the groups. The results suggest that the banking sector increased the nominal amount of bail-inable bonds issued by riskier banks relative to safer banks, while other financial institutions decreased their holdings.

The increase in the amount of bail-inable bank bonds held by the banking sector impairs financial stability. At the same time, market discipline did not increase, since other (sophisticated) financial intermediaries and the non-financial corporations sold securities of the riskiest banks. Overall, the cases of bank distress did not improve the allocation of bank bonds. The danger to financial stability persists as the banking sector increased the amount held of risky bonds by increasing the risk of contagion in case of a bank failure, while, at the same time, the retail sector did not significantly change its portfolio allocation.

References

Avgouleas, E., & Goodhart, C. (2015). Critical reflections on bank bail-ins. *Journal of Financial Regulation, 1*, 3–29.

Banco Santander Confident on Banco Popular After 'Stabilizing' It. (2017). *SNL*. https://www.snl.com/web/client?auth=inherit#news/article?id=41465616&KeyProductLink-Type=6. Accessed 12 October 2018.

Crespi, F., & Mascia, D. (2018). Bank funding strategies. *Palgrave Macmillan Studies in Banking and Financial Institutions.*

Fiordelisi, F., Minnucci, F., Previati, D., & Ricci, O. (2020). Bail-in regulation and stock market reaction. *Economic Letters, 186.*

Keister, T. (2016). Bailouts and financial fragility. *Review of Economic Studies, 82*, 704–736.

O'Hara, M., & Shaw, W. (1990). Deposit insurance and wealth effects: The value of being "too big to fail." *The Journal of Finance, 45*, 1587–1600.

Pancotto, L., Gwilyim, O., & Williams, J. (2019). The European bank recovery and resolution directive: A market assessment. *Journal of Financial Stability, 44.*

Philippon, T., & Salord, A. (2017). Bail-ins and bank resolution in Europe: A progress report. *Geneva Reports on the World Economy Special Report 4.*

Santos, T. (2017). El Diluvio: The Spanish Banking Crisis 2008–2012, https://www.dnb.nl/en/binaries/Tano%20Santos_tcm47-360757.pdf. Accessed 7 May 2018.

Shafer, A., Schnabel, I., & di Mauro, B. W. (2016). Bail-in expectations for European banks: Actions speak louder than words. *ESRB Working Paper Series.*

CHAPTER 5

Market Reactions to Resolution Events

Abstract The long period (from 2011 to 2019) wherein several instances of bank resolution resulted in bailout or bail-in allows to analyze how financial markets reacted. Using this relatively long time span and the different resolution events, a comparison of market reactions can be made according to the type of the event (e.g. bailout and bail-in) and the uncertainty surrounding its implementation. We analyzed the abnormal stock prices returns through event studies. The analysis shows a negative impact on the stock price returns following resolution cases regardless of the resolution mechanism implemented. The financial market reacts negatively when the resolution is undertaken within a bailout framework, but the reaction is smaller in absolute value when compared with bail-in resolution cases. However, after the formal approval of the bail-in regulation, investors began to react less negatively to bail-in resolution cases than to bailouts.

Keywords Abnormal returns · Bail-in · Bailout · CAR · Bank resolution

A. M. Maddaloni and G. Scardozzi, *The New Bail-In Legislation*, Palgrave Macmillan Studies in Banking and Financial Institutions, https://doi.org/10.1007/978-3-030-87560-2_5

5.1 Introduction

The Bank Recovery and Resolution Directive (BRRD) introduced the new resolution regime. The main innovation was that, starting January 1, 2016, the resolution of a European bank could no longer entail the use of taxpayers' money (bailout) while the bail-in mechanism would apply. However, the BRRD contains an article on precautionary recapitalization (article 32.4) that allows liquidity injections by the government under specific conditions. Government liquidity cannot be used to cover losses, and the instruments to be used are contingent convertible bonds. This provides some room for flexible implementation of the resolution regime. There have been cases (discussed in Chapter 4) wherein liquidity injections were implemented.

Before the bail-in directive came into force, some failing banks were resolved through a bail-in mechanism because of the limited fiscal capacity of national governments, especially during the recession period after the financial crisis and affecting in particular the countries with high sovereign debt (Greece, Ireland, Italy, Portugal, and Spain, briefly GIIPS countries). As these governments were not in the financial condition to bail out stressed financial institutions, they applied the bail-in mechanism. However, the mechanism had yet to be prescribed by the law (see the case of Bank of Cyprus in 2013).

The occurrence of these distress events constitutes an opportunity for researchers to study the reaction of equity holders in order to primarily understand whether the new resolution mechanism is perceived to be credible by the market and to understand the extent to which the different types of resolution may cause capital flight.

Equity holders are sensitive to any bank resolution, both via bailout (Fratianni & Marchionne, 2013) and bail-in (Shafer et al., 2016). Several studies analyze the reaction in the literature following the dates of the bail-in regulation and its application (see Crespi & Mascia, 2018; Cutura, 2018; Fiordelisi et al., 2020; Giuliana, 2019; Pancotto et al., 2019). Scardozzi (2021) comprehensively analyzes equity holders' different reactions after bank resolution by comparing the type of the event (bailout or bail-in), the time of the event (before or after the approval of the BRRD), and the failing bank's country. This chapter analyzes equity holders' reactions to a series of resolution events in the European Union by assessing the credibility of the new resolution tool among equity holders and more importantly by evaluating the possibility of capital flights after resolution events. Capital flights constitute, in fact, another critical side effect of the new EU resolution regime.

We collect a series of bailout and bail-in events from 2011 to 2019. By analyzing abnormal returns on European banks' stock prices, we assess the equity holders' reactions to different resolution cases, running an event study. The analysis provides insights on whether the bail-in mechanism caused less abnormal reactions by equity holders than the bailout; whether the implementation of the new resolution regime has implications on bank equity valuation; and whether the country where the failing bank is located still matters, notwithstanding the implementation of a common EU framework for the resolution of banks. We found that, in general, equity holders reacted worse to bail-in resolutions than to bailouts; this behavior reverted after the approval of the BRRD suggesting that the bail-in events became less unexpected. Finally, analyzing the home country driver, it turns out that the abnormal returns following the resolution of banks in peripheral countries were less negative than the abnormal returns after the resolution of banks in core countries with wider fiscal capacity. Overall, the evidence suggests that expectations are a very important factor in determining investors' reactions to such events.

5.2 Summary of the Resolution Cases

This section reports a summary of the bank resolution cases that occurred in Europe from 2011 to 2019.

Amagerbanken: The Amagerbanken's headquarters were in Denmark. The bank fell in distress in 2009, and it received some government capital injections. In 2011, it was declared bankrupt (February 6, 2011), and an additional bail-in of senior debt and unsecured depositors was implemented. Senior debt holders and unsecured depositors covered 110 million euros of Amagerbanken losses.[1]

Bankia: Bankia, in Spain, fell in distress in July 2012. After some recapitalization, on July 10, 2012, the bail-in of subordinated debt became necessary to cover around 30% of the losses.

Monte dei Paschi di Siena: Monte dei Paschi di Siena (MPS), in Italy, has been in financial trouble since 2012. The European Commission approved state aid on December 17, 2012, for 3.9 billion euros due

[1] https://ec.europa.eu/info/sites/default/files/dp011_en.pdf.

to the possible threat to financial stability as MPS is the third-largest bank in Italy. The state aid recapitalized MPS, increasing its Common Equity Tier 1 in compliance with the request of the European Banking Authority (EBA). This event can be classified as a bailout.

SNS Reaal: SNS Reaal is a bank from The Netherlands. The bank suffered heavy write-downs of its real estate portfolio in 2012, and on February 1, 2013, the Dutch government nationalized it. The government injected 2.2 billion euros of new capital, and the bail-in was applied for equity holders and junior creditors. One billion of subordinated debt was also wiped out in the operation.[2]

Bank of Cyprus: The bank has been under resolution since March 18, 2013, with the Central Bank of Cyprus acting as the resolution authority. The resolution applied the bail-in tool. Uninsured depositors (for deposits above the insurance threshold of 100,000 euro) were bailed-in by converting 47.5%[3] of their deposits into equity. Bondholders and equity holders covered the losses as well.

The Co-operative Bank: This is a UK bank where a "consensual" bail-in among the bank investors was carried out. Bondholders were converted into equity holders for 1.5 billion pounds, avoiding any use of taxpayers' money (bailout). The bail-in was agreed upon and implemented on June 17, 2013.

Hypo Group Alpe Adria: Hypo Group Alpe Adria (HGAA) is an Austrian bank. Since 2008, HGAA received state aid and was nationalized in 2009. On September 3, 2013, the European Commission agreed to implement a reconstructing plan for HGAA using taxpayers' money.

Slovenian banks: This case refers to a group of Slovenian banks that fell under the resolution procedure. The group was composed of Nova Kreditna Bank, Maribor (NKBM), Nova Ljubjanska Banka (NLB), Probanka, and Factor Banka. On December 20, 2013, the Slovenian government injected 3 billion euros for their recapitalization.

FIH: FIH is a bank located in Denmark; its resolution pertains to the several bailouts implemented by the Danish government. After several liquidity injections since 2012, on March 11, 2014, the European Commission approved a decision in favor of its nationalization.

[2] Shafer et al. (2016).

[3] https://ec.europa.eu/info/sites/default/files/dp011_en.pdf.

Eurobank Ergasias: Eurobank Ergasias is located in Greece. On April 29, 2014, state aid was provided to the bank in common shares, and contingent convertible bonds issued to the government-owned Hellenic Financial Stability Fund borrowed from the European Stability Mechanism.

Allied Irish Bank: Allied Irish Bank (AIB) resides in Ireland. The bank was one of those in trouble after the 2007 financial crisis. State aid has been provided to AIB, and on May 7, 2014, the European Commission approved a rescue plan to recapitalize AIB. The bailout of AIB cost around 9.5 billion euros.[4]

Alpha Bank: Alpha Bank is a Greek bank. Together with the National Bank of Greece and Piraeus Bank, it benefited from the biggest rescue plan approved by the European Commission for Greece via the recapitalization in state aid. Specifically, the decision to provide state aid for Alpha bank occurred on July 9, 2014.

National Bank of Greece, Piraeus Bank: These are two Greek banks that, as previously described, belong to the Greek group of banks recapitalized through state aid. The European Commission decided to recapitalize these two banks a few days after the Alpha Bank decision, on July 23, 2014.

Banco Espirito Santo: In 2014, Banco Espirito Santo (BES) was the third-largest banking group in Portugal, being, therefore, a systemically important institution. Bank of Portugal forced BES to provide a restructuring plan that the European Commission then approved. The resolution consisted of splitting the bank in two on August 3, 2014. The BES remained a "bad bank" where equity holders and subordinated bondholders were written down against the bad assets, senior bondholders, and depositors were, instead, transferred to a "good bank," Novo Banco. This action may be classified as a bail-in type of resolution.[5]

Hypo Group Alpe Adria: Since 2009, Hypo Group Alpe Adria (HGAA) was in financial troubles because of bad loans granted to its borrowers. The bank was first nationalized and then it was reorganized maintaining the good assets into HGAA and creating a vehicle bank "HETA" (publicly controlled) where the non-performing assets were

[4] https://www.pai.ie/bank-bailout-costs-state-nearly-e42-billion/.

[5] https://ec.europa.eu/info/sites/default/files/dp011_en.pdf.

transferred. On October 30, 2014, the Austrian government decided to implement the bail-in of subordinated bond holders.

Panellinia: Panellinia is a Greek bank. On April 17, 2015, the Bank of Greece resolved Panellinia by transferring part of its assets and liabilities to Piraeus Bank, while the equity holders were bailed-in.[6]

Andelskassen: On October 5, 2015, the Danish Andelskassen JAK Slagelse Bank was resolved. Assets and liabilities were transferred to a bridge bank, and all investors were fully bailed-in except for covered depositors fully protected by the Danish Guarantee Scheme.

National Bank of Greece: National Bank of Greece (NBG) was one of the four main Greek banks. On October 30, 2015, subordinated and senior bondholders of NBG were bailed-in by converting their bonds into equity.

Small Italian banks: The resolution of small Italian banks includes the cases of Banca Etruria, Cassa di Risparmio di Ferrara, CariChieti e Banca delle Marche. Equity holders and subordinated bondholders were bailed-in on November 30, 2015. This resolution episode is very well known because many of the subordinated bondholders were retail investors that endured particularly large losses.

BANIF: On the December 19, 2015, BANIF was resolved, the main business was sold to Banco Santander Totta. Equity holders, and subordinate bondholders were bailed-in.

Heta Asset Resolution: The Austrian bank was born from the rescue of HGAA. The resolution of Heta Asset Resolution bailed-in the subordinated bonds and part of the senior bonds on April 10, 2016.

HSH Nordbank: HSH Nordbank is a bank located in Germany. Since June 2013, the bank had been in distress; the rescue plan involved substantial state aid during the following years, and on May 2, 2016, the European Commission finally approved the increased Government guarantee granted to the bank in June 2013. Since the notification of the decision to resolve HSH Nordbank dated back to 2013, the resolution of the bank did not fall under the BRRD framework, and a bailout was implemented.

Banco Popular Espanol: This is the first and full bail-in applied after the bail-in provision became effective. Banco Popular was a Spanish bank, and the ECB declared the institution was failing or likely to fail with

[6] European Parliament (2016).

the consequent approval of the resolution procedure under the BRRD framework on June 7, 2017. No state aid was provided to the failing institution.[7]

Veneto Banca, Banca Popolare di Vicenza: These two Italian banks were declared failing or likely to fail by the ECB in the same month that Banco Popular insolvency took place (June 23, 2017). However, in this context, the Single Resolution Board decided that these two banks were not of public interest and that their resolution should be implemented under the national insolvency proceedings, with Bank of Italy as the responsible authority. In spite of the BRRD, the Italian government granted state aid to the failing banks. Still, the liquidation implied the bail-in of equity holders and subordinated bondholders.[8]

Banca Carige: Banca Carige resides in Italy as well. On January 10, 2019, the Italian government decided to inject liquidity into Banca Carige to restore their capital. No bail-in has been implemented.

Nord LB: This is a German bank struggling due to the excessive amount of non-performing Loans. On December 5, 2019, a public resolution plan was approved by the European Commission. This event can be classified as a bailout event. While the bail-in regulation was already in force at the time of resolution, the bank's crisis started before the regulation became effective.

Table 5.1 summarizes these events, classified as bail-ins in those cases where the bail-in tool has been applied fully or partially. In those cases where the bail-in was not applied, and the resolution involved only public interventions, the events have been classified as bailouts.

5.3 Empirical Analysis

From the analysis on equity holders' reactions to bank resolution events, it is possible to distinguish three different effects: the effect caused by the type of resolution applied (bailout or bail-in), the effect determined by the date of the event (before or after the approval of the BRRD), and the effect specific to the home country of the failing bank.

First, the analysis compares market reactions following the two different types of resolution events, regardless of the date in which they

[7] See Chapter 4 for more details.

[8] See Chapter 4 for more details.

Table 5.1 Bank resolution cases

Name of the bank	*Country*	*Date*	*Type of the event*
Amagerbanken	Denmark	02/07/2011	Bail-in
Bankia	Spain	07/10/2012	Bail-in
Monte dei Paschi di Siena	Italy	12/17/2012	Bail-out
SNS Reeal	The Netherlands	02/01/2013	Bail-in
Bank of Cyprus	Cyprus	03/18/2013	Bail-in
The Co-operative Bank	United Kingdom	06/17/2013	Bail-in
Hypo Group Alpe Adria	Austria	09/03/2013	Bail-out
Slovenian banks[a]	Slovenia	12/20/2013	Bail-out
FIH	Denmark	03/11/2014	Bail-out
Eurobank Ergasias	Greece	04/29/2014	Bail-out
Allied Irish Bank	Ireland	05/07/2014	Bail-out
Alpha Bank	Greece	07/09/2014	Bail-out
National Bank of Greece, Piraeus Bank	Greece	07/23/2014	Bail-out
Banco Espirito Santo	Portugal	08/04/2014	Bail-in
Hypo Group Alpe Adria	Austria	04/30/2014	Bail-in
Panellinia	Greece	04/17/2015	Bail-in
Andelskassen	Denmark	10/05/2015	Bail-in
National Bank of Greece	Greece	11/02/2015	Bail-in
Small Italian banks[b]	Italy	11/23/2015	Bail-in
BANIF	Portugal	12/21/2015	Bail-in
Heta Asset Resolution AG	Austria	04/11/2016	Bail-in
HSH Nordbank	Germany	05/02/2016	Bail-out
Banco Popular Espanol	Spain	06/07/2017	Bail-in
Veneto Banca, Banca Popolare di Vicenza	Italy	06/23/2017	Bail-in
Banca Carige	Italy	01/10/2019	Bail-out
Nord LB	Germany	12/05/2019	Bail-out

Note The table shows the bank resolution cases that happened from 2011 to 2019. [a]Slovenian banks are: Nova Kreditna Banka Maribor (NKBM), Nova Ljubljanska Banka (NLB), Probanka and Factor Banka. [b]The small italian banks are: Banca Etruria, Cassa di risparmio di Ferrara, CariChieti and Banca delle Marche
Source Scardozzi (2021)

occurred and the home country of the failing bank. The aim is to assess whether bail-in events caused worse equity holders' reactions than bailout resolution cases. In general, bank crises induce a negative reaction of the market. However, the reaction may vary, at least in magnitude, according to the tool applied for resolving the failing bank (bailout or bail-in). Bailout events are generally perceived negatively by investors. Panetta et al. (2009), for example, show the negative effect of state aids on equity prices, which might be due to the dilution of capital after this type of resolution is implemented.

Second, the analysis aims to shed some light on the role of market expectations. More specifically, the assumption is that events in which the current regulation was not applied may have caused larger equity holders' reactions. For instance, one might expect that, before the approval of the BRRD, the bail-in events caused a negative reaction, larger in absolute value, because they were unexpected. The opposite could be true for bailout events after the approval of the directive. The introduction of the BRRD should have reduced equity holders' expectations of future state interventions in bank resolution cases. The role of the expectations could even prevail on the effect determined by the type of the event.

Finally, we analyze the role of the expectations comparing the reactions by home country. The goal is to understand whether investors react differently if the bank belongs to a country in which the sovereign has a worse financial position (such as Greece, Italy, Ireland, Portugal, and Spain) than other EU countries. In particular, we will assess whether bail-in resolution events of banks headquartered in countries with a stronger financial position implied stronger equity holders' reactions because they were more unexpected.

To implement the analysis, we use the same dataset exploited in Scardozzi (2021) containing stock prices from January 1, 2011 to December 31, 2019, collected from Thomson Reuters Datastream with daily frequency. The sample includes all the listed European banks for which the data are available. The event study analyses the "abnormal" stock return (AR) around the resolution event, calculated as the difference between the actual stock return and the return predicted by the market model. The market model (MacKinlay, 1997) estimates the normal return for every firm as a function of the market portfolio return. The parameters of the market model are the daily log-returns of stocks and the EUROSTOXX600 index representing the market portfolio over a 252-day estimation period ending 20 days before the date of the event.

$$\mathrm{AR}_{i,t} = R_{i,t} - (\alpha + \beta R_{M,t}) \tag{5.1}$$

Table 5.2 Summary statistics—full sample

Total	*Mean (%)*	*Min (%)*	*Max (%)*
CAR(−1,1)	−0.21	−42.66	50.93
CAR(−3,3)	−0.46	−50.06	36.39
CAR(−5,5)	−0.47	−63.42	71.95
Bail-in			
CAR(−1,1)	−0.18	−42.66	50.93
CAR(−3,3)	−0.65	−50.06	35.51
CAR(−5,5)	−0.98*	−63.42	71.95
Bail-out			
CAR(−1,1)	−0.25	−29.35	26.47
CAR(−3,3)	−0.23	−40.46	36.39
CAR(−5,5)	−0.17	−43.78	40.15

Note The table reports the means of the Cumulative Abnormal Returns (CARs) aggregated into symmetric time windows. In the group "Total," there are the means and the statistical significance of the returns registered for the whole sample, the minimum value, and the maximum value. The sub-groups are "bail-in," which includes the CARs registered after the resolution cases that applied the bail-in, and "bailout," which is complementary. The sample includes the stock prices of all European listed banks excluding the banks in crisis (listed in Table 5.1). *,**,*** represent the statistical significance at 1%, 5%, and 10%, respectively
Source Scardozzi (2021)

The banks' resolutions events that we analyze occurred from 2011 to 2019. These resolution events applied a bailout or bail-in mechanism. Moreover, these events occurred before and after the approval of the new European directive on the harmonization of resolution practices (BRRD).

The ARs, once calculated, have been aggregated for symmetric time windows in terms of days: (−1,1), (−3,3), (−5,5). For each time window, the abnormal returns are then cumulated into Cumulative Abnormal Returns (CAR).

The analysis studies the CARs, aggregated into different groups, to understand the overall reaction of equity holders to the resolution events examined. Table 5.2 shows the summary statistics for CARs.

Table 5.3 Summary statistics—failing banks

Total	*Mean (%)*	*Min (%)*	*Max (%)*
CAR(−1,1)	−1.68**	−64.27	26.47
CAR(−3,3)	−3.46**	−135.10	70.45
CAR(−5,5)	−3.46**	−162.93	40.17
Bail-in			
CAR(−1,1)	−2.12*	−64.27	26.47
CAR(−3,3)	−5.29**	−135.10	70.45
CAR(−5,5)	−5.74*	−162.93	40.17
Bail-out			
CAR(−1,1)	−1.08	−29.35	15.30
CAR(−3,3)	−0.93	−40.46	24.46
CAR(−5,5)	−0.28	−41.38	35.89

Note The table reports the means of the Cumulative Abnormal Returns (CARs) aggregated into symmetric time windows. In the group "Total," there are the means and the statistical significance of the returns registered for the whole sample, the minimum value, and the maximum value. The sub-groups are bail-in, which includes the CARs registered after the resolution cases that applied the bail-in, and the bailout group, which is complementary. The sample includes the stock prices of the failing banks listed in Table 5.1. *,**,*** represent the statistical significance at 1%, 5%, and 10%, respectively
Source Scardozzi (2021)

The results show the means of the CARs with symmetric time windows. They generally have a negative pattern, which is larger in absolute value for cases of bail-in resolution. The equity holders reacted more negatively to the resolution cases where investors needed to cover the bank losses with their capital.[9] We restrict the sample only to failing banks and calculate similar summary statistics. Table 5.3 shows the results.

A reaction worse than the one in Table 5.2 emerges from the analysis. From a financial stability point of view, the resolution of a financial institution caused a contagion effect by generating negative abnormal returns also for other financial institutions that were not in distress before.

[9] These results come from a sample that excludes the failing banks from the date of their resolution onwards.

Overall, the financial market reacted negatively to the resolution cases, although, as expected, the equity holders reacted worse.

Although these results are not statistically significant, the variability is huge. A natural step forward in the analysis is to move into a multivariate setting that simultaneously considers different events' different features. The regression model implemented is the following one:

$$\text{CAR}_{i,t} = \alpha + \beta_1\text{BAIL\_IN}_{i,t} + \beta_2\text{BRRD}_{i,t} + \beta_3\text{BAIL\_IN} * \text{BRRD}_{i,t} + \beta_4\text{Same\_Country}_{i,t} + \beta_5\text{GIIPS}_{i,t} + \beta_6\text{Euro}_{i,t} + \varepsilon_{i,t} \quad (5.2)$$

where the dependent variable is the cumulative abnormal return for the bank i in day t; among the independent variables, BAIL_IN is a dummy equal to 1 when the resolution of the failing bank was a bail-in and 0; otherwise, BRRD is a dummy equal to 1 for the resolution events after the approval of the BRRD (April 15, 2014) and 0 otherwise. The choice to use the directive approval date rather than its entry into force in 2016 is due to the market's possible anticipatory behaviors, as outlined by Fiordelisi et al. (2017) and Fiordelisi et al. (2020). The two dummies have interacted with each other, and BAIL_IN*BRRD considers the bail-in resolution events after the approval of the BRRD directive. Three other independent variables are then included in the model to account for differences among countries: Same_Country, GIIPS, and Euro. The former is a dummy equal to 1 if the bank i belongs to the same country of the failing bank. The second is a dummy equal to 1 for the banks belonging to countries with a sovereign in weaker financial position (Greece, Ireland, Italy, Portugal, and Spain); the dummy Euro equals 1 for banks in the Euro Area and 0 otherwise.

Table 5.4 shows the results of the regression model.

The coefficient of BAIL_IN is negative and statistically significant at a 5% level in all the windows. The multivariate analysis suggests that the resolution events to which the bail-in tool applies generate a worse reaction from the financial market than bailout events. We can argue that bail-in events caused worse equity holders' reactions than bailout resolution cases. Although equity holders perceived all the resolution events negatively regardless of the tool applied, this analysis finds that, between the two tools, the losses covered using investors' money generated worse financial reactions than state aids. The type of tool applied has, therefore, a clear effect on the magnitude of market reactions.

Table 5.4 OLS regression

Variables	*CAR(−1,1)*	*CAR(−3,3)*	*CAR(−5,5)*
BAIL_IN	−0.005*	−0.013***	−0.023***
	(0.002)	(0.003)	(0.004)
BRRD	−0.001	−0.002	−0.001
	(0.002)	(0.003)	(0.004)
BAIL_IN*BRRD	0.008***	0.014***	0.018***
	(0.003)	(0.004)	(0.005)
Same_Country	0.003	0.001	−0.001
	(0.003)	(0.005)	(0.006)
GIIPS	0.000	0.005**	0.004
	(0.001)	(0.002)	(0.003)
Euro	−0.004***	−0.007***	−0.009***
	(0.001)	(0.002)	(0.002)
Constant	0.000	0.000	0.005
	(0.002)	(0.003)	(0.003)
Observations	3264	3264	3264
R-squared	0.007	0.014	0.020

Note The table reports the results of the regression model. The dependent variable is the CARs aggregated into the symmetric time windows. *,**,*** represent the statistical significance at 1%, 5%, and 10%, respectively

Source Scardozzi (2021)

The BRRD dummy is not statistically significant but negative anyway. It is interesting to observe the coefficient of the interaction between the two dummies: BAIL_IN*BRRD. In all the time windows, the coefficient is positive and statistically significant at a 1% level, showing the primary role of investors' expectations regarding the financial market's reactions. From the approval of the new resolution tool, which clearly states that the bank losses should be covered with investors' money rather than taxpayers' money, equity holders reacted less negatively to banks' resolution cases applying the bail-in mechanism. This is because they were more predictable than the government injecting liquidity into the failing bank despite the clear prohibition by the directive. These results show that the bail-in is credible from the investors' point of view, which supports the SRM goals of market discipline, which should limit the sovereign bank nexus. Moreover, it wards off capital flights and the contagion effect thanks to clear rules for resolution. However, we note that the magnitude of the coefficient BAIL_IN partially offsets the above-mentioned coefficient BAIL_IN*BRRD: the overall result indicates that after the regulation approval, the equity market reactions were more muted.

The geographical determinants show interesting results. The dummy Same_Country is never statistically significant: the resolution cases do not generate larger reactions for banks in the same country than for other European banks. This supports the view of globalized and interconnected financial markets. Moreover, the variable GIIPS has a positive coefficient even if weakly significant; only the time window (−3,3) is statistically significant at 5% level. This means that the market reactions to cases of bank resolutions in countries with a weaker sovereign financial position were negative but smaller in absolute value than those in financially sound European countries. A possible explanation for this result relies on the country's fiscal capacity. Shafer et al. (2016) show that in countries with a weaker sovereign financial position, such as Greece, Ireland, Italy, Portugal, and Spain, the expectations of a bank bailout are more limited. Conversely, in countries with ample fiscal capacity, bail-in resolutions are more unexpected and generate a greater reaction on the financial markets. Finally, the model includes the dummy variable Euro. Its coefficient is negative and statistically significant at 1% in all three-time windows. The common currency can explain the financial market's reaction to the resolution cases that were worse when involving banks belonging to the Euro Area. The common currency seems to induce a greater contagion effect.

5.4 Conclusion

The financial market's reaction to an exogenous shock is the topic of a large literature, most recently also including the reactions to the exogenous shock brought upon by the COVID-19 pandemic. For the scope of this analysis, the cases of bank resolution constitute a quasi-natural experiment to test the effect of the change in resolution regimes implemented by the policymakers after the global financial crisis. The huge amount of state aids provided by the national governments to banks in trouble contributed to an extended sovereign debt crisis in the Euro Area. The implementation of the BRRD introduced a bail-in framework and established a hierarchy of the banks' investors.

This chapter provided a comprehensive analysis of the financial market's reaction to bank resolution cases involving bailout and bail-in tools. The analysis studies the abnormal stock price return through an event study using bank resolution cases in the EU from 2011 to 2019.

The time sample is long enough to include both bailout and bail-in resolutions, occurring before and after the approval of the new directive and in countries with different fiscal capacities.

The analysis shows a negative pattern in the stock price returns following resolution cases regardless of the resolution mechanism implemented. The financial market reacts negatively also when the resolution is undertaken within a bailout framework. Still, the reaction is smaller in absolute value than for bail-in resolution cases. However, after the formal approval of the BRRD, investors began to react less negatively to bail-in resolution cases than to bailouts. This means that the new resolution tool is deemed credible by the market, improving market discipline. The role of investors' expectations is primary in this framework.

Finally, from a spatial point of view, the analysis shows that the banks belonging to the Euro Area have registered worse abnormal stock returns than in other European countries, suggesting that the common currency amplifies the contagion effect.

It is important to observe that the analysis was carried out in a context of non-systemic crises with limited contagion effects. Nevertheless, the results suggest a benefit arising from the implementation of a clear resolution framework, which overall may increase the resilience of the banking system in the face of large, exogenous shocks, as the COVID-19 pandemic.

References

Crespi, F., & Mascia, D. (2018). Bank funding strategies. *Palgrave Macmillan Studies in Banking and Financial Institutions.*

Cutura, J. (2018). Debt holder monitoring and implicit guarantees: Did the BRRD improve market discipline? *SAFE Working Paper Series n.232.*

Fiordelisi, F., Minnucci, F., Previati, D., & Ricci, O. (2020). Bail-in regulation and stock market reaction. *Economic Letters, 186*, 108801.

Fiordelisi, F., Ricci, O., & Stentella Lopes, F. S. (2017). The unintended consequences of the launch of the Single Supervisory Mechanism in Europe. *Journal of Financial and Quantitative Analysis, 52*, 2809–2836.

Fratianni, M., & Marchionne, F. (2013). The fading stock market response to announcements of bank bailouts. *Journal of Financial Stability, 9*, 69–89.

Giuliana, R. (2019). Impact of bail-in on banks bond yields and market discipline. *SSRN*. https://doi.org/10.2139/ssrn.2935259

MacKinlay, A. C. (1997). Event studies in economics and finance. *Journal of Economic Literature, 35*, 13–39.

Mesnard, B. (2016). "Bail-ins" in recent banking resolution and State aid cases. *European Parliament 7 July 2016.*

Pancotto, L., Gwilyim, O., & Williams, J. (2019). The European bank recovery and resolution directive: A market assessment. *Journal of Financial Stability, 44*, 100689.

Panetta, F., Faeh, T., Grande, G., Ho, C., King, M., Levy, A., Signoretti, M., Tbapga, M., & Zaghini, A. (2009). An assessment of financial sector rescue programmes. *BI Occasional Paper, Questione di Economia e Finanza, Banca d'Italia.*

Scardozzi, G. (2021). Reazioni di mercato agli eventi di risoluzione bancaria. *Banca Impresa e Società, 40*(2), 271–290.

Shafer, A., Schnabel, I., & di Mauro, B. W. (2016). Bail-in expectations for European banks: Actions speak louder than words. *ESRB Working Paper Series.*

CHAPTER 6

Conclusion

Abstract The change in bank resolution policy in Europe generated some "unintended" consequences on the financial system with both positive and negative connotations. The new European banking resolution regime fosters financial stability by increasing the banking sector's resilience, necessary to withstand the occurrence of strong exogenous shocks like the COVID-19 pandemic. In this manuscript, we review some of the consequences of the transition from a bailout to bail-in resolution. We observe, firstly, a change in the bank liability mix toward cheaper sources of funding (such as customer deposits). Then, we analyze the reallocation of banks' bonds holdings; before the approval of the new resolution regulation, mis-selling of risky bank bond was widespread, but after the implementation of the bail-in mechanism, there was a reallocation of bank bonds toward more sophisticated financial intermediaries. Finally, we analyze the market reactions at the bank resolution events.

Keywords Unintended consequences · Bail-in resolution · Bank bonds

A. M. Maddaloni and G. Scardozzi, *The New Bail-In Legislation*, Palgrave Macmillan Studies in Banking and Financial Institutions, https://doi.org/10.1007/978-3-030-87560-2_6

6.1 Conclusion

The global financial crisis showed that even the failure of a single bank could have enormous global implications. In Europe, the implementation of the European Banking Union (EBU) project has played a pivotal role in preserving the stability of the banking sector and the financial sector at large.

The EBU is composed of three pillars. The first created a common system for the supervision, the second pillar harmonized the resolution of European banks, and the third pillar aims to improve and harmonize the deposit guarantees at European level. Among these three pillars, the second pillar is the focus of this manuscript. The second pillar was formalized with the Bank Recovery and Resolution Directive (BRRD); it aims to enhance orderly bank crisis management once banks have been declared as failing or likely to fail by the European Central Bank. Specifically, the new resolution framework prescribed four resolution tools: among them, the one that deserves more attention is the bail-in tool. The bail-in sets a hierarchy among the liability instruments of banks to bear the losses of the failing banks, instead of injecting liquidity by the Government (e.g. bailout), hence using taxpayers' money.

In this book, we reviewed some of the "unintended" consequences of the changes in banking resolution policy in the EU. The transition from a bailout to bail-in resolution implied that bank losses would have to be covered using investors' rather than taxpayers' money. This should have led investors to ask for a greater risk premium on their investments, thus increasing the cost of funding for banks. We observe that such an increase, already well documented in the literature, may also induce a change in the bank liability mix. Indeed, the increase in the cost of funding for banks was not equal for all banks' funding sources. Investors generally asked for a higher risk premium for bank liabilities less protected by the new resolution directive, in particular bonds. Bank deposits remain at the bottom of the bail-in hierarchy and are in part also insured by national Deposit Guarantee Schemes (DGS). We observe that after the BRRD announcement, banks changed their liability mix toward cheaper sources of funding. They increased the portion of customer deposits relative to other interest-bearing liabilities (constituted mainly by bonds). While deposits represent a relatively stable source of funding during non-crisis times, there are concerns that excessive reliance on bank deposits increases asset-liability mismatch and increases liquidity risk, especially when shocks occur. The occurrence of an exogenous shock like the COVID-19 pandemic represents a stress scenario for the banking system. The economic downturn induced by the restrictive measures due to the pandemic induced an increase in the liquidity need of both households and corporations. Banks may face significant liquidity shortages since deposits can be withdrawn without limits and with almost no notice.

The second dimension of analysis that we addressed in the book relates to the reallocation of banks' bonds holdings across different sectors due to the bail-in. After several mis-selling scandals happening in the EU during 2012–2013, it has been recognized that the pursuit of financial stability should also imply a coherent allocation of risk across holders' sectors. Retail investors do not seem to be the right targets for bank bonds (especially after the introduction of the bail-in regime) because they are mainly interested in investing their lifetime savings. Further, they lack the financial literacy needed to evaluate these instruments correctly. It would be advisable that banks limit their holdings of these securities as well to avoid a cascade effect in case of a bank failure. Other financial intermediaries (e.g. non-bank) have the financial sophistication suitable for such investments; further, they have a more speculative behavior. We show that before the approval of the new resolution regulation mis-selling was widespread, especially in some southern Euro Area countries. From 2010 to 2014, households mainly held speculative-grade bonds. After establishing the bail-in mechanism, there was a reallocation of bank bonds from households to other (non-bank) more sophisticated financial intermediaries. At the end of 2019, before the COVID-19 pandemic, bank bonds in Euro Areas were mainly held by the two most financially sophisticated sectors (i.e. banks and other financial intermediaries). In terms of consumer protection, this allocation may be seen as an improvement compared to the situation before the new resolution regime. However, policymakers may want to limit the holdings of banks' bonds by the banking sector to avoid contagion risk and systemic crises in case of a bank failure. The cross-selling (banks holding other banks' bonds) is a potential threat to financial stability under the new bail-in regulation.

The reallocation of bank bonds across sectors may have been a direct consequence of the episodes of bank distress resolved in the EU under the new bail-in regime. The analysis shows that the banking sector increased its share of holdings of bank bonds issued by relatively riskier banks; simultaneously, other (sophisticated) financial intermediaries sold bonds issued by relatively riskier banks. This result highlights a serious concern for financial stability because contagion risks in the banking sector have increased after the implementation of the new resolution regime.

Finally, Chapter 5 provides evidence concerning the market reactions at the resolution events. We show how abnormal returns of banks' equity prices can be identified around the resolution cases involving both bailout and bail-in. The bail-in tool is deemed credible by the market, improving market discipline. We also show that the BRRD approval resolved some of the market participants' uncertainty related to banks' resolution, limiting the potential contagion effect due to capital flights. However, the common currency amplifies the contagion effect. More negative reactions have been found by Euro Area investors than those in other European countries.

Overall, the change in resolution policy generated some "unintended" consequences on the financial system with both positive and negative connotations. The new European banking resolution regime fosters financial stability by increasing the banking sector's resilience, particularly when strong exogenous shocks like the COVID-19 pandemic hit the system.

Index

A. M. Maddaloni and G. Scardozzi, *The New Bail-In Legislation*, Palgrave Macmillan Studies in Banking and Financial Institutions, https://doi.org/10.1007/978-3-030-87560-2

The manufacturer's authorised representative in the EU is Springer Nature Customer Service Centre GmbH, Europaplatz 3, 69115 Heidelberg, Germany. If you have any concerns regarding our products, please contact ProductSafety@springernature.com

Printed and bound by CPI Group (UK) Ltd, Croydon, CR0 4YY
30/09/2026
02225475-0002